A Left-Hand Turn Around the World

A Left-Hand Turn Around the World

Chasing the Mystery and Meaning of All Things Southpaw

DAVID WOLMAN

Da Capo Press
A Member of the Perseus Books Group

Design and composition by Trish Wilkinson
Set in 12-point Goudy

Library of Congress Cataloging-in-Publication Data

Wolman, David.
    A left-hand turn around the world : chasing the mystery and
meaning of all things southpaw / David Wolman. — 1st Da Capo
Press ed.
        p.   cm.
    Includes bibliographical references and index.
    ISBN-13: 978-0-306-81415-0 (hardcover : alk. paper)
    ISBN-10: 0-306-81415-3 (hardcover : alk. paper) 1. Left-
and right-handedness. I. Title.
GN233.W65 2005
152.3'35—dc22   2005022387

First Da Capo Press edition 2005

Published by Da Capo Press
A Member of the Perseus Books Group
www.dacapopress.com

Da Capo Press books are available at special discounts for bulk
purchases in the U.S. by corporations, institutions, and other
organizations. For more information, please contact the Special
Markets Department at the Perseus Books Group, 11 Cambridge
Center, Cambridge, MA 02142, or call (800) 255-1514 or
(617) 252-5298, or e-mail special.markets@perseusbooks.com.

    1   2   3   4   5   6   7   8   9—08   07   06   05

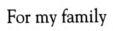
For my family

Contents

Preface

I have been interested in women's feet.[1]

—*45-year-old Ichiro Irie, after his arrest for stealing
the left shoes of two hospitalized women in the Japanese
town of Usa. After searching his house, police
discovered a collection of 440 left shoes.
Why the bias for the left remains unclear.*

A woman asked me last night what I plan to do in Left Hand, and what exactly this book of mine is about. My response was unusually concise: if you could commit a year to explore the world of left-handedness, where would you go, whom would you meet, and what would you learn?

To begin my quest, I posed the following question to a number of leading scientists: if left-handedness were a religion, where would Mecca be? Within reason, I tried to visit all of the places they came up with, as well a few locations of my own devising. Much of the research for this book has been an effort to find answers to the specific questions of what causes left-handedness and how left-handers might differ from the right-handed majority. Yet at the risk of sacrificing continuity, I've also permitted spontaneity to sit shotgun, influencing many of my reporting and itinerary decisions. My thinking was that a journey isn't much of a journey if it follows a straight, predictable path.

As a left-hander, I've long since suspected, or at least wondered, whether handedness, left- or right-leaning, might be more than a frivolous idiosyncrasy. But never could I have anticipated that pursuing the origins and consequences of left-handedness would lead me to larger, indeed some of the largest, scientific questions of our time, such as the origins of language and the evolution of the modern mind, to say nothing of the subject's link to such famous thinkers as Plato, Charles Darwin, Carl Sagan, Stephen Jay Gould, Noam Chomsky, and Albert Einstein.

There are theories out there asserting how this or that overlooked animal or unassuming object changed the world, saved the world, altered the course of history, or rescued modern civilization. Such a prominent role for handedness, and left-handedness in particular, is probably a stretch. Yet the motivation behind this book springs from a similar curiosity about something seemingly small that exploded into a broader exploration, launching me on an adventure that would lead to a castle in Scotland, monkeys in Atlanta, neuroscientists in Berkeley, golfers in Japan, psychologists in London, an amputee in Illinois, palm readers in Quebec, and brains in Paris.

The result of this around-the-world reporting is either a testament to how diverse—and fascinating—the subject of handedness truly is, or a confirmation of just how far off the deep end I've gone with this Southpaw stuff. My hope is that the experiences and personalities encountered along the way will resonate in ways that make you think a little more about handedness—and in ways that never occurred to you before.

David Wolman
Left Hand, West Virginia
October 16, 2004

CHAPTER 1

The Chosen People

Perhaps the moment is uniquely
propitious for the left hand . . . [1]

———————

—Jerome S. Bruner,
On Knowing: Essays for the Left Hand

I have an obsession with left-handedness. Noticing all
things Southpaw is simply part of my programming. It's
not that I'm just a journalist with an overflowing file of lefty-
related clippings. My interest in this topic, unlike other cu-
riosities that seem to come and go with each edition of the
Sunday paper, has lasted longer than any other I've ever
had, with the notable exception, presumably, of my right-
handed wife.

Why is it that I remember things like driving past the
Lefty Golf Shop on Williston Road in Burlington, Vermont,
perhaps 10 years ago, yet I can no longer remember the qua-
dratic equation? Why is it that I remember the Leftorium in
an old *Simpsons* episode; the town of Left Hand, West Virginia; the Left Hand Brewery in Colorado; and the hand
preference of all my friends? This is the mental clutter that

has accumulated in my brain. Years ago, an Irish friend told me that *ciotóg*, pronounced, "ki-toeg," is Gaelic for "lefty." I learned a lot of Gaelic words and phrases that summer in Ireland, but the only two I remember to this day are *ciotóg* and *póg mo thoin*, or kiss my ass.

One time while in Japan, I was actually stupid enough to say to the barber, perhaps in a desperate attempt to put my beginner Japanese language skills to work: "Hey, you're a lefty. So am I." Already flustered by having a *gaijin* in his shop, this guy must have really been taken for a ride by my comment. Staring at me for a few moments before lifting his scissored hand into the air, he said tersely, "No. It's the mirror." Ten bucks says he still tells this story at parties.

The thing is, though, most lefties are pleased to bond with a fellow Southpaw, even if for a nanosecond. As soon as I see a waiter pull pen from apron with the left hand, you can bet on some lefty-style greeting coming from me. Before others at my table have glanced at the appetizer menu, I've already taken a quick survey of whether the waiter prefers the seizure-esque, tensed-up, hooked-hand posture; the impossibly odd, slanted-notepad approach; or the rare pen and paper position that actually looks normal—in the righty sense of the word—indicating a grammar school teacher of extraordinary genius and sensitivity.

I'll see a Southpaw and often say something like, "Southpaw—nice," or, "Lefties—gotta love 'em." Righty readers might find this to be a foolish, superficial ploy for a free beer, and although the complimentary beverage may happen on occasion, that's not the goal. You see, lefties just understand this exchange in a way righties cannot because the fraternity of Southpaw is something that can only be known from the inside. A friend in college once snapped at me when I pestered him about why on Earth he participated in a fraternity: don't knock what you can't understand, he said. As goofy as lefty greetings may sound, nine out of ten times they are well received, often eliciting one of a handful of responses, such as, "We're just better," or, "Right brain, baby," or the most common of all, "You know it."

The lefty superiority complex that gives rise to such asides as "We're just better" did not emerge randomly but rather is the result of eons of prejudice, ridicule, and neglect. For instance, at a friend's wedding a few summers ago, seated in a perfect row of white chairs, behind the perfectly white and green exterior of the Equinox Hotel, which sits in the perfectly green setting of Manchester, Vermont, I listened to the words of a genteel Justice of the Peace as he told the groom to take the bride's right hand, and repeat the following. Inside my head: "The right hand? Why the right hand? There it is again; example No. 76,466 of the subtle, entrenched, unfair dominance of the damned right hand!" Instead of speaking out, though, I chose to hold my tongue and not interrupt the wedding to voice my frustration. You have to pick your fights. If I ever have to testify in court, that oath-taking moment could be an opportune time to bring up this concern. I'll raise my left hand and place my right hand on the Bible and see what happens.

Deciding where to sit at a dinner table with friends—now there's an occasion for a little venom. Whereas I used to sheepishly let others determine who's to sit where, adopting a Zen-like, peaceful-warrior approach to social interaction, I've since overhauled my policy. Now I decide, declaring that I should sit here, gesturing toward a corner seat and promptly sitting. (Round tables, by the way, are nice for the conflict-avoider-type personality.) By taking hold of the reins, I prevent someone else from launching into an annoying presentation about who should sit where and how to account for the standout lefty. Don't kid yourselves, Southpaws. There's some deep disapproval embedded in the whole "let's accommodate for the lefty" thing, especially if it's topped off with a little chickeny elbow dance. For those who find these exchanges intolerably annoying, I recommend telling the group it's really no big deal and that you sometimes eat with your right hand. Then, during the meal, proceed to eat with your left hand, purposefully jabbing the person to your left.

It's true that we Southpaws complicate the calculus of table seating and have trouble using fountain pens. But what's been bugging me for years, and what's motivated this quest, is the mystery of what causes left-handedness; what makes us different from the righty majority; and what, if anything, unites us?

If I were forced to declare association with a group of "ists" or a set of believers, I would probably declare myself a humanist, then a journalist, then a Red Sox fan-ist. Technically, my people are the Jews, but religion has never done it for me. The only subset of humanity I have ever really enjoyed identifying with is the legion of left-handers. Maybe that makes me a humanist with lateral bias. I don't think a Parisian, a Palestinian, or a Presbyterian is any better or worse than I am, has any less or more insight into the human condition than others, or has more plausible explanations for life's unanswerable mysteries than anyone else. But if that Parisian, Palestinian, or Presbyterian is one of the

10–12 percent of the people on Earth who happen to be left-handed, she's slightly more interesting to me than the other 88–90 percent.

I grew up the only lefty among four siblings. For as long as I can remember, being a Southpaw was a source of pride. My right-handed parents excelled at encouraging the lefties-are-special shtick, perhaps to boost my self-esteem as a middle child. I ate it up. Through the ages, I've owned a couple of left-handed mugs, numerous pairs of left-handed scissors, birthday cards that open from the left, and a bumper sticker that reads: "Lefties never miss at toll booths." I also had a navy blue T-shirt emblazoned with the ultimate Southpaw cliché: "If the right side of the brain controls the left side of the body, then only left-handed people are in their right minds!"

I learned early on that when it comes to sports, Southpaws have noticeable advantages. Even the very term "Southpaw" apparently derives from baseball, most likely coined in Chicago in the late nineteenth century. Left-handed pitchers on the mound at the old Comiskey Park would face west, so that the arc of their arm and delivery of the ball originated from the south. One source suggests that a *Chicago News* sportswriter invented the term, although a different source claims that it was used to describe left-handed boxers before it was applied to left-handed pitchers.[2] Today, "Southpaw" is frequently used in such sports as boxing and tennis but is by far most pervasive in baseball.

Lefties, so they say, throw a natural curveball, and in my years of little league and into high school, I put this theory to the test, trying to throw a curve that would, by the very nature of my nature, be that much more vicious. Roy Hobbs could do it in *The Natural*; Bruce Hurst could do it for the '86 Red Sox; and countless other famous lefty hurlers had the curve to beat any batter. Why should I be denied that fame? Because I couldn't consistently throw the ball over home plate to save my life. During one little league game, I hit the same opposing batter in three of his four at-bats. My future as a star Southpaw pitcher dimmed quickly.

Tennis had similar potential advantages but served up a familiar outcome for me. Left-handed tennis players confuse opponents because their forehand and backhand are the opposite of what most people are used to facing. Advantage-court serves in particular can, with enough coordination and ferocity, fly impossibly off the side of the court, like those delivered by John McEnroe or Goron Ivanisevic, the giant Croat who, when he finally won Wimbledon in 2001, celebrated a few days later by stripping down to his underwear in front of 150,000 fans in his hometown of Split, Croatia. You have to hand it to lefties—or at least to towering, Croatian, left-handed tennis stars—they're not boring.

My problem as a kid tennis player was that I double-faulted all the time. Still do. But every now and then I manage to put the ball in the proper service box and capitalize on the lefty factor. It's usually the result of a miss-hit, yet when the ball bounces with unexpected spin, handcuffing my opponent with confusion, I try my best to act like the shot was hit exactly according to plan. Rare as they are, those shots are hugely rewarding, especially for such a galactically frustrating game as tennis. A successful serve offers one of those moments, not unlike watching Southpaw Rocky Balboa in any of the *Rocky* movies, when I think: man, is it cool to be left-handed.

Cool if for no other reason than because it means being different. As an upper-middle-class white kid in an uppity Boston suburb, being left-handed helped, in its own minuscule way, fend off the ominous prospects of mediocrity. My grades were B-range, my haircut was like most other kids', my athletic skills were nothing more than fine, my artistic abilities were average, I couldn't dance or sing, and my upbringing was comparatively uneventful, lacking ample drama for a future, heart-wrenching memoir. But at least I was a lefty.

Yet how does that really make me different, aside from the obvious smudged writing and supposed natural curveball? This journey, an exploration into the essence of Southpaw, will help to answer that question.

CHAPTER 2

The Bend Sinister

That raven on your left-hand oak
(Curse his ill-betiding croak)
Bodes me no good.[1]

—John Gay

O n a recent travel writing assignment in Moscow, I was walking past the Kremlin and turning onto Vozdvizhenka Street when I stumbled upon an ad hoc weekend market full of farmers from the countryside selling honey, cashews, slightly dirty apricots, and other foods from their gardens.

I had my notepad out and was jotting down a few thoughts when all of a sudden a giant, blonde, card-carrying *babushka* in a huge navy blue wool sweater, with an even more huge voice, came charging up to me, gesturing wildly with her left hand. Through my translator, she explained that it was bizarre to see someone writing with the left hand, and the laughter from the other merchants indicated she wasn't alone in this impression. I tried to talk with her about Russian views of handedness, but she just kept pinching my cheeks, rubbing my hair, and suggesting that I come back to the countryside with her, where she would find me a sweet young Russian wife.

In many parts of the world, the hand we use for certain activities is an indicator, like skin color, used to identify, stratify, or prejudge. Most people presume the hand used for writing is the litmus test for determining whether someone is lefty or righty, and for anyone content to live with a pedestrian level of knowledge on the subject, this narrow reading will serve well enough. But if you bought this book, or if you were given this book, chances are you're game for a bit more specificity.

Everyday tasks, like throwing and eating, also influence the popular understanding of hand dominance, sometimes nearly as strongly as writing. These different behaviors lead immediately to a quintessential problem of handedness inquiries: how to define handedness itself. The definition of lefty or righty varies, sometimes to a frustrating degree, and that variation has troubled researchers who want to get a better handle on why it is that humans have hand preference and performance discrepancies in the first place, where these discrepancies come from, and why as a population we usually favor the right hand.

Imagine a hypothetical study in which you've been asked to investigate whether left-handed people, disproportionate to their overall numbers within a population, like eating pineapples. To conduct the study you could ask a group of people signing in somewhere—at a PTA meeting, on a university campus, in a doctor's office—to check a box next to their names indicating left- or right-handedness, and then another box for pineapple like or dislike.

The problem is that millions of people all over the globe have, as children, a natural tendency to write and eat with the left hand but because of cultural bias are taught, if not forced, to use the right hand instead. This trend, though more prevalent in the past, persists in many parts of the world today, especially in poorer countries where one hand is designated for eating and the other for, ahem, hygiene. How people report their own handedness varies.

The reverse situation, though less common, is also possible. People who use the right hand for two or three essential skills may report that they're right-handed, even though they use the left hand preferentially for a number of other tasks. As a result, respondents in the pineapple study who're similar in their handedness could provide contradictory answers, sending your investigation to the scrap heap. Take a 60-year-old man who at the age of 5 was switched from writing with his left hand to writing with his right, and now he writes, eats, and plays racquetball with the right hand—is that man a right- or left-hander?

Another challenge in defining handedness arises from varying definitions and intractable stigmas about handedness within different cultures. Whereas people in North America generally perceive writing to be the primary indicator for handedness status, people in some Asian countries believe eating is the key sign of a lefty or righty. And in cultures where left-handedness is considered lesser or sinister, why would someone admit to being left-handed? All of these pitfalls explain why asking individuals if they're left- or right-handed won't suffice; you can't compare measurements of something if the definition of that something varies

within your sample group of self-reporting, notoriously falli-
ble humans.

For the purposes of this book and most modern-day psychology and neuropsychology research into handedness, a
dependable, or at least dependably workable, definition of
right-handedness goes like this, with due thanks to Michael
Corballis of the University of Auckland, who is one of today's high priests of laterality research. Someone who's right-
handed prefers "the right hand for most tasks requiring a
single hand, and the right hand dominates in tasks involving
both hands, such as unscrewing the lid of a jar."[2] Left-handers
are generally the opposite.

Currently, experts believe that about 10–12 percent of
the human population is left-handed, with slightly more
lefty men than women. Yet the global figure of 10–12 percent comes wrapped in caveats. For starters, the survey instrument of choice, the Edinburgh Handedness Inventory
(EHI), isn't perfect; instead of checking one box to indicate
handedness, respondents are asked to check ten boxes. The
test was developed in the 1970s to get a sharper understanding of respondents' handedness than was possible with
simple, one-question self-reporting. Although often tweaked
this way or that, the barebones version looks like the figure
on the next page.

From tallies of this questionnaire, researchers calibrate
what they call the *laterality quotient*, which is basically a form
of the score that's easier to crunch through the machinery of
statistics. To be sure, the EHI has limitations and bias. One
scientist I spoke with laughed when recalling how, the first
time he took the EHI as a graduate student, he reported
that he brushed his teeth with his right hand. At home that

Edinburgh Handedness Inventory

INSTRUCTIONS: Indicate your preference in the use of the hands for the following activities:			
	Left	*Right*	*Either*
1. Writing			
2. Drawing			
3. Throwing			
4. Scissors			
5. Toothbrush			
6. Knife (without fork)			
7. Spoon			
8. Broom (upper hand)			
9. Striking match (match)			
10. Opening box/lid			

Source: Oldfield, R. C., "The Assessment and Analysis of Handedness: The Edinburgh Inventory." *Neuropsychologia* 9 (1971):97–113.

night, he realized he was in fact a lefty brusher. Nevertheless, many studies about hand preference nowadays use the EHI, or some variation on the same theme, to gauge hand dominance for major tasks and thus the incidence of left- and right-handedness across sample population groups.

But while the EHI was designed to assess differences in hand preference, other tests target differences in hand *performance*. Sometimes the hand we prefer is not necessarily the superior performer, a fact that often jumps to mind when my right-handed wife holds the steering wheel with only her left hand, at which point I say a silent prayer that she's indeed more of a lefty than she realizes. One major tool of the trade for calibrating dexterity is a pegboard test. The setup of one type, the Purdue Pegboard, has two parallel rows of 30 holes. At one end sit a concave dish of small metal pegs and another dish holding tiny metal donuts. The idea is to use one hand and, as quickly as possible, pick up and place individual pegs down one row of holes, then do so again with the other hand. After that, do the same for the little donut rings, placing them over each peg. A researcher standing by with a stopwatch tracks the times, and most people will perform better with the dominant hand.

Unlike the pegboard, the benefit of the EHI is that it works on a sliding scale, with people scoring, for instance, 7 out of 10 in favor of right-handedness. Yet for investigating possible correlations between handedness and a certain trait or behavior, be it a taste for pineapple, high SAT scores, or susceptibility to allergies, EHI respondents are always plunked down in either the left- or right-handed category. Those who score 5–5 or 4–6 might be included in a separate, third category of mixed-handers, or they may be excluded from the end results so as not to confuse a study bent on, and perhaps funded for the purpose of, looking at lefties versus righties. That trend is changing, as I'll explain in a later chapter, but for the most part the scientific literature continues to embrace the lefty-righty dichotomy.

Mixed-handed people, by the way, are not ambidextrous. Mixed-handed means exactly what it implies, preferring one hand for some everyday tasks and the other hand for others. In common usage, "ambidextrous" has become a frequent substitute for mixed-handed, though the strict definition is equal dexterity with either hand for all tasks, a condition that is quite rare, perhaps one or two people in 1,000. Truly ambidextrous people would check "either" for all questions on the EHI, and some scientists argue that no one is absolutely ambidextrous. That doesn't change the anti-lefty bent of the term, though, translated from Latin as literally "two rights."

All the varying types of handedness, definitions of the word, and inadequacies of survey instruments aside, 10–12 percent of the population is the number to take to the bank, for now. That's us, left-handers. Were we to form our own political organization, we would have an unparalleled volunteer force for canvassing and a huge war chest of soft-money contributions. Were we to form an official religion (unofficially, some of us already have), we would comprise one of the most popular in world history. Should we decide to form our own country, the Democratic Republic of Southpaw would be the planet's third most populous nation after China and India, placing us solidly in the running for the medals title at the Olympics.

But so far, about the only things that seem to unite Southpaws are a history of being put down and judged as evil, awkward, or lesser by the insecure majority and being the focus of scattered snippets of science and pseudoscience that, although intending to provide insight, often end up confusing more than clarifying.

In the Western world, left-handedness has long been associated with the worst of the worst: sin, devil worship, Satan himself, and just an all-around bad position with God. Catholic schoolteachers used to tell students that left-handedness was "the mark of the Beast," the Scots say a person with terrible luck must have been baptized by a left-handed priest, and orthodox Jews wrap their left arms in the leather strap of *tefillin* as if to say, in the words of Rabbi Lawrence Kushner: "Here I am, standing with my dangerous side bridled, ready to pray."[3] The Bible is full of references to hands, and usually they are about God doing something benevolent and holy with his right hand. I'll spare you the run-through and stick to a token example, like this one from Psalms 118: "The right hand of the Lord is exalted. The right hand of the Lord doeth valiantly."

From an etymological perspective, the roots of the word *left* are just about as depressing as it gets. The Anglo-Saxon *lyft* means weak or broken, and even modern dictionaries include such meanings for *left* as "defective," "crippled," "awkward," "clumsy," "inept," and "maladroit," the latter one borrowed from French, translated literally as "bad right." Most definitions of *left* reduce to an image of doubtful sincerity and clumsiness, and the Latin word for left, *sinister*, is a well-known beauty.[4] From this version springs my favorite term for left-handedness, "the bend sinister,"[5] which Vladimir Nabokov used for the title of a book[6] that has nothing to do with handedness.* If I ever own a Hummer, a massive hunting rifle, or something else sufficiently huge and obnoxious, I think I'd like to call it "The Bend Sinister." An Oregon winery even has a blend named the Sinister Hand,

---

*According to Nabokov's 1964 introduction to the book: "The term 'bend sinister' means a heraldic bar or band drawn from the left side (and popularly, but incorrectly, supposed to denote bastardy). This choice of title was an attempt to suggest an outline broken by refraction, a distortion in the mirror of being, a wrong turn taken by life, a sinistral and sinister world."

derived from an Irish legend about someone who got his left hand chopped off. I know, I know. All of this talk of being inept and klutzy sounds ridiculous. As if anyone could make an argument that the likes of Martina Navratilova, Larry Bird, and Steve Young are maladroit. Yet this kind of label barely scratches the surface of the anti-leftedness infecting language and culture worldwide. I'm not just talking about surfing or snowboarding stances that are either "regular" for righty style or "goofy" for lefty style. This stuff runs deep.

How deep? Writing at the turn of the twentieth century, a German anthropologist traced the cause of the right hand's exalted status to prehistoric religions and symbolism about left and right drawn directly from nature. For example, facing a rising sun to the east and following its course through the sky puts the sun on the viewer's right-hand side (for people in the northern hemisphere). "There is an intimate link between the dominant right hand and the movement of the sun, that giver of life and warmth," writes laterality scholar Chris McManus.[7]

It's not difficult to find symbolic associations between the left and attributes or phenomena such as bad, inferior, death, and ghosts, whereas the right is usually linked to the sacred, prosperity, and benevolent spirits. Carl Sagan hypothesized that the association between left and bad emerged because of the left hand's use for hygiene purposes in nonindustrialized countries, but it's likely the stigma existed long before this practice.

Reading a recent article from a scientific journal, I found that researchers—in fact the very people who study the genetics, neurology, and psychology of handedness—had no problem using the term *sinistrals* to describe left-handed people.[8] Need a few more examples from the anti-lefty language front? How about "born from the left side of the bed" for a child born out of wedlock, a "left-handed marriage" for an adulterous act, "left-handed wisdom" for faulty reasoning, and a "left-handed wife" meaning a mistress or someone who obviously lacks *right*eousness.

The grand prize in the annals of anti-lefty lingo, however, has to go to a 1950s study in Great Britain cataloging colloquialisms for left-handedness in different parts of the country. The list of 87 terms is hilarious in its entirety, but the quick, R-rated sampler includes: skivvy-handed, scrummy-handed, kaggy-fisted, cawk-fisted, gibble-fisted, and cunny- and ballock-handed. A smart sportscaster somewhere could have a field day with these descriptors.

Of course, "left" and "right" have their political connotations too. Stanford University linguist Geoffrey Nunberg traces this fluid distinction from revolutionary France, across the Atlantic, and into the fire-breathing mouths of McCarthyites, who used "leftist" as a descriptor for Communist sympathizers. In the late 1990s, the term *leftist* saw a revival, although it also underwent a notable shift in meaning:

> In 1954, the Girl Scouts of America was labeled a leftist organization when the American Legion and the House Committee on Un-American Activities accused it of permitting a former Communist to serve as a troop leader and of using a handbook that preached "UN and World Government propaganda." When the leftist charge is repeated now, it's because the scouts permit lesbians to be troop leaders and support programs like Title IX, the law that expanded opportunities for girls and women in U.S. sports.[9]

More recently, notes Nunberg, the modified label of "liberal-leftist" has emerged, a hybrid term not unlike "toaster-oven." Meanwhile, politicos on the right, while not too fond of "right wing," have been clever to stay relatively stationary on the spectrum of political labels, not necessarily because the word's double entendre promotes the idea that their views are correct, although that surely can't hurt their efforts.[10]

Then again, that the word *left* shares an etymological bed with *sinister, clumsy, defective,* or Thin Mint cookies, even though interesting and a noteworthy point of connection for Southpaws, probably doesn't merit a march on Washington. And yet this theme of left-handers as an oppressed, oft-neglected population not only underlies much of the popular dialogue on the subject but also is frequently used to justify academic efforts. On a recent visit to the Handedness Research Institute at Indiana University, for instance, I ran into a small poster with pictures of 15 or so different desk chairs, all right-biased in their construction. The title on the poster read: "100 years of Desk Bias at Indiana University," and on the bottom the tagline read, "Don't Institutionalize Discrimination. Buy Unbiased." The rest of the institute offices were either locked or empty, and the only person I could connect with was an elusive associate professor who refused to meet me in person, suggesting maybe the population at large, including most Indiana lefties, don't find society's right-hand desk bias to be that oppressive.

Not that the point about discrimination is completely without merit. On my way to the airport for the trip to Indiana, for example, my Eritrean cab driver said that in his homeland, no one is allowed to eat with the left hand, and if they do, the older people will hit them. The guy even demonstrated a smack by whacking his own hand atop the steering wheel. A few weeks later, a friend told me about a man she met in Uganda who, watching her write with her left hand, said if he ever caught his wife writing with her left hand he would divorce her. And through the Handedness Research Institute I did manage to exchange email with an Indian contact named Bipinchandra Chaugule, who's writing a "guide for parents and teachers of left-handed children in India," where harsh bias against left-handedness is prevalent.

The time has come, I think, not to gripe about inequity but rather to embrace fully the way of the left-hander. Perhaps our quirky penmanship, our advantage in baseball, and the notion of our mental prowess—even if it's incorrect—all serve us well. It is time to celebrate left-handedness.

With so many people on the planet, I figured this idea might have occurred to others before me, so I began looking around for groups exalting all things Southpaw. That search led me to something called the Left Hand Path, and an unusual left-hander right here in Portland.

———— • ◆ • ————

Diabolos Rex: "8:00 P.M. will be fine. But I won't know how to recognize you."

"People say I look like Ferris Bueller."

Rex: "OK. Well, I don't think you'll miss me. See you tonight."

With that, I'm set for my rendezvous with the self-appointed Devil King. Left-hander Diabolos Rex is Megister Templi for the Church of Satan, meaning he's roughly equivalent to a head cardinal in the Vatican, though Catholics might take umbrage at the parallel. On a pink blossom April evening, I sit alone in a nearly empty bar, pretending to read the newspaper because I want to appear casual, yet looking up every 35 seconds.

Suddenly he's in the doorway, a complete human being, even though at first all I see are two horns and a beard. Rex smiles, we shake hands, and he apologizes for being late. I'm in such disbelief about the horns pressing skyward from under his scalp—and what I see upon further inspection to be an inch-long trident implanted between his eyebrows—that I can barely put together a don't-worry-about-it response.

Rex has a shaved head. He wears black from his cape collar to his boots, a pentagram pendant, and a long, dual-pointed black beard. Large silver rings affixed to his lower lip arc downward like thin tusks. I try as hard as possible not to stare at the rippled, 4-inch, horn-shaped implants that jut upward from his spiky black eyebrows.

Although I'm here to talk about left-handedness and the Left Hand Path, the horns are like conversational tractor beams. Rex, charitably, doesn't mind: "They're medical grade Teflon implants." His "implant specialist" cut thin holes atop his head, pried open a space within the subcutaneous tissue, and then inserted the horns.

Eventually we turn to the Left Hand Path. Originating from Eastern religions, the idea is that the Buddha—without ever having read a Robert Frost poem about diverging roads in the woods—opted for the leftward, less common path, which was then pioneered, at least in the eyes of Satanists, by those who opposed the ascetical approach to life prescribed by most major religions. Church of Satan goers are quick to point out a frequent misperception: they don't worship Satan. They employ the word *satan* to describe the skeptical, questioning, adversarial position of being forever contrary to Judeo-Christian theology. Satanists are "I-theists," viewing each person as a primary centerpiece in her own universe. The Right Hand Path, by contrast, "is about suppression of lust and carnality and transcending the material world. We think that's more of a spiritual pipe dream," says Rex.

During Church of Satan ceremonies, the left hand plays a leading role. The rationale, aside from a sort of literal homage to the Left Hand Path, is that the left hand is so consistently overlooked, if not scorned by the dominant religions of the world—have you ever seen someone cross himself with his left hand?—exalting, or even just occasionally utilizing the left hand is another way to oppose mainstream religion. That Satanists use the left hand not because of their own belief in its inherent quality but only to contradict the beliefs and rituals of others admittedly limits this minor victory for the greater cause of Southpaw pride. But beggars can't be choosers and frankly, when it comes to preferential attention doled out to the left hand, I'm buying from whoever's selling.

What does the Left Hand Path mean to Rex? "To me it's just the path. My perspective is completely separate from what they see." "They," presumably, are Right Hand Path takers and possibly right-handers. "Satanists are an ethnicity or race," he says, beginning one of his high-speed stretches of verbiage. "The orientation of the psyche is what classifies one as a Satanist. It is pure action, and it is my conviction that you either are that way from birth or you aren't. Like being left-handed . . . The Left Hand Path is

Truth that's representing the one opposed to the masses. We deal with our own realities."

Perhaps because Rex is an artist, he hones in on the matter of writing and penmanship. "The right-handed person gives us insectoid, conformist, lockstep, assembly-line letter creation," which sounds more than a little contrived for my benefit, but I like it anyway. "They slavishly drag the hand and letters across the page. But the left-hand point of view, like in writing, is creation. Pushing forward."

Stroking his beard, Rex declares: "Left-handed people are more emotional, intuitive, and more often into occults. The left hand is feminine, darkness, and water. The right hand is daylight, solid, and masculine." I nod now and then, but to be honest I mostly think about how painful the implants look and what aspects of the self this guy and I could possibly share beyond left-handedness. What Rex doesn't have, unfortunately, is much of a sense of Southpaw pride. "To do so means I'd want to be connected to other people. But I believe in my own island," he says, which I probably should have guessed in light of Satanism's "I-theist" philosophy.

Still, he's interested enough. "David, your task is to find out if left-handed people are spiritually or mentally different from right-handed people and if so, is that improved evolution or somehow retrograde, devolution."

He isn't exactly the Oracle to my Hercules, but Rex's charge is pretty much on target, and, dare I confess, energizing. But before I can delve into the question of difference, I've got to try to uncover the origins of left-handedness. As it turns out, the hunt for tangible answers begins in the brain. Two nineteenth-century brains, to be precise, both of them entombed in a Paris museum.

CHAPTER 3

Broca's Brains

The Old Brain was remote and mysterious,
deeply hidden within the skull and inaccessible . . . [1]

—*Richard Restak, MD*, The New Brain

T he clouds below look like the rippled, winding surface of
a brain, and as the plane descends toward Paris I imagine I'm inside a tiny molecule, orbiting, then diving into the
vast terrain of cerebral gray matter. The next morning at
5:00 A.M., jet-lagged beyond reason and sick of watching
CNN, I venture out into the January drizzle, heading north
on Hemingway's beloved Boulevard Saint-Michel toward
the Sorbonne and the brains made famous by Paul Broca.

Born in 1824—150 years to the day before me—French
surgeon and scholar Paul Broca may be the closest thing the
religion of Southpaw has to a prophet. He was a leader in
medicine, anthropology, and later politics, but it was his
work on the brain that earned Broca a spot alongside other
French titans of discovery like Pasteur, Curie, and Cousteau.
Inside every person's head, usually on the left side, is a region of the brain known today as Broca's area.

I've come here, to the Left Bank of the Seine, to pay my re-
spects at Broca's grave in Montparnasse, stroll through some
of his old turf in the Latin Quarter, binge on the same types of
pastries he once ate, and, most of all, check out two brains in
the morbid anatomy collection at the Dupuytren Museum.

Before time-warping to the nineteenth century, a quick
primer: It's a well-known aspect of the brain-body relationship that control of movement is crisscrossed. That is, the
act of swatting at a buzzing mosquito with the right hand is
controlled by the left side of the brain, or more specifically
by a certain area of the left hemisphere known as the left
motor cortex, which sends the necessary signals to muscles
in the right arm. The reverse is true for actions carried out
with the left hand, and all of this is irrespective of handedness. The hemisphere on the same side as a movement isn't
entirely silent, as I'll discuss later, but for the most part motor control comes from the opposite hemisphere.

This contralateral control, first described by Hippocrates
himself, isn't limited to hands.[2] It applies to arms, legs, eyes,
ears, and indeed almost all motor faculties, which is why
people who've had a stroke or tumor on one side of the
brain often experience partial or total paralysis on the opposite side of the body. Why our brains and bodies are cross-
wired in this manner is a whole other mystery, although
observation of this phenomenon still provides an important
clue to the roots of handedness.[3]

The left and right sides of the brain are physically quite
distinct. The brain is made up of two mostly separate halves,
each composed of billions and billions of neural connections.
Yet despite popular notions to the contrary, left-handed
people do not think in the right hemisphere of the brain, nor

do right-handers think in the left hemisphere. The motor cortex, that part of each hemisphere cross-wired to control the other side of the body, is only one relatively minor aspect of this dizzyingly complex organ, and it says nothing or nearly nothing about a person's thoughts or personality. Nor does handedness mean that the right hemisphere of righties is napping whenever right-handers perform left-sided movements, or vice versa for lefties.

Our two seemingly independent brains are able to work together because they aren't totally isolated from each other. Picture the brain as a melon mostly sliced in half, but with a stringy bundle of tissue still connecting the two halves in the middle. This bundle of nerve fibers running between the two sides of the brain is called the corpus callosum. The two hemispheres are also anchored together at the brain stem, but it's the bridging corpus callosum across which huge volumes of information pass back and forth. Beyond these two details—the cross-wired brain and the connector role of the corpus callosum—there's no need to be weighed down with more brainy lingo.

In mid-nineteenth-century Europe, neurology was just being born. Surgeons, anthropologists, biologists, and other scientists gathered in Paris to debate what could or couldn't be understood about the nature of humankind based on analysis of the brain and surrounding structure. It was dangerous intellectual turf due in part to the steady influence of quack practices and in part to the ubiquitous pressure of the church and religious leaders. Darwin had just dropped the "E-bomb" in 1859, and scientists exploring the inner workings of the brain were easy targets for those in power firing off accusations of blasphemy.

Proceeding cautiously, Broca and other members of the *Société Anatomique, Académie de Médecine,* and the *Société d'Anthropologie,* the latter of which Broca is credited with founding, wanted to make sense of recent evidence suggesting patients with damage to a certain region of the brain suffered from similar deficits of language. It was 1861 when two particular patients were first brought to Broca's attention.

———•◆•———

The streets of Paris gradually awaken, with garbage collectors, sweeping shopkeepers, and a few people scurrying toward bakeries to deliver baguettes and croissants. After a few hours wandering and sampling espressos in the Latin Quarter, I find the museum entrance in a quiet courtyard just off the Rue de l'Ecole Médecine. An elderly gentleman in a sweatshirt answers the bell, and I step into what looks like a discombobulated laboratory from Broca's day: A long desk crowded with specimens in cylindrical glass jars; leatherbound books stacked horizontally; piles of wrinkled papers; and old wooden and brass scientific instruments. After the old man finds his keys, he leads me into the museum, which is just a large room with a red floor. To my relief, it doesn't smell like rotting, 200-year-old flesh.

Black- and gold-trimmed glass cases line the walls and are filled with more than 6,000 jarred nineteenth-century specimens, skulls, and molds. Just about anything one could think to put in a medical museum dedicated to morbidity and freakiness is here: eyeballs; mice with their guts hanging out; molds of grossly deformed faces; aborted fetuses; a double uterus; skeletons of feet; hands; wickedly curved spines; a mold of an abdomen with a hernia the size of a watermelon; tumors; kidneys; organs split in two and displayed like two halves of a geode; other malformed reproductive organs; and disfigured, Siamese, even "tri-amese" babies that are sure to have starring roles in my next nightmare.

The case at the far end of the room holds over a dozen brains. The two belonging to Broca's patients are the museum's most famous items, though fame is a relative term when places like Notre Dame Cathedral and the Louvre are just up the street, and aside from two other visitors in the museum, I'm alone with the brains.

The first one sits upright in a cylindrical jar of fluid—formaldehyde, alcohol, and who knows what—that's yellowy and somewhat murky. The folds of the nearly 200-year-old brain have glommed together somewhat and lost their distinctiveness. But the damage to the left frontal lobe is still clear, or more accurately the negative space of the lesion is there, its cavity revealing even to the untrained eye that something was wrong with this brain.

It belonged to a man identified as "Tan," so named for the only utterance he was capable of producing. His real name was Leborgne. An epileptic who first began noticing weakened control of his right side in his thirties, Leborgne slowly lost more motor function over the years, as well as his sight and some of his mental faculties. By the time Broca examined him shortly before his death at age 51, Leborgne had also lost the capacity for speech.[4]

That Leborgne could understand spoken language but could not articulate speech was a paramount curiosity, and Broca was not the only clinician to take notice of this unusual condition. The rule of contralateral motor control had already come into focus, so Leborgne's partial paralysis wasn't a newly observed symptom either. Where Broca broke away from the pack was in synthesizing Leborgne's inability to speak; his impaired sensitivity on the right side of his body; his active left hand, observed when Leborgne tried to gesture his way through communication; and the pathology of his brain.[5]

Soon after Leborgne died, Broca performed a postmortem and found massive damage to the front left portion of his brain, perhaps caused by a tumor, although the "basic disease has never been satisfactorily diagnosed."[6] Piecing the case history together with what he saw in Leborgne's brain, Broca tentatively concluded that a link existed between the damaged area of the left hemisphere and the inability to speak. He also decided against plunging his surgical tools deeper into Leborgne's brain, confident that he'd gleaned enough by observing the obvious lesion to the left frontal lobe of the cerebral cortex and believing instead that the specimen belonged in a museum. "He sensed its historical role," writes biographer Francis Schiller. Broca put the brain in a jar.[7]

The second brain is that of an elderly man named Lelong. Although it was removed and preserved the same year as Leborgne's, for whatever reasons of positioning, chemical proportions within the liquid, or possibly the quality of the lid's seal, Lelong's brain is in significantly better condition. Resting horizontally in a rectangular jar reminiscent of a flask without a spout, the brain is an ash shade of gray, the lines and lobes so clearly defined that the specimen looks more like a clay model sculpted two years ago than an actual brain of someone who lived 200 years ago.

Lelong had come to the hospital after a bad fall and could say only a handful of words. He died two weeks later. When

Broca examined Lelong's brain, he found a lesion of the left hemisphere in the same place as it had been in Leborgne's brain—"rigorously" so, as Broca put it—only this time it was more concentrated in the region that would later become known as Broca's area.[8] The lesion is still obvious today and more contained than that of Leborgne's brain.

From the case histories of Leborgne and Lelong, followed by corroborating evidence gathered over the next few months, Broca was able to demonstrate convincingly that the left hemisphere of the brain is dominant for various language faculties and that a certain area of the left-frontal lobe is the seat of articulate speech. More broadly and of primary interest for the question of handedness, Broca had shown that the hemispheres of the brain differ in significant and seriously interesting ways.[9] The unevenness of hand preference begins with the unevenness of the brain, and when it comes to the story of brain asymmetry, Broca opens Act I.*

Broca zoomed in on the relevant area of the left hemisphere associated with speech deficits and made it impossible to ignore the anatomical reality of an uneven brain

---

*A few decades earlier, a French doctor named Marc Dax living near Montpellier had written an unpublished paper linking the inability to speak with damage to the left side of the brain. Dax would not get his due until years later when his son posthumously published his father's remarkable work. Twentieth-century writers sifting through details about dates of publications, correspondences, and interactions between different individuals have tried, in a sometimes-noble, sometimes-quibbling effort, to identify precisely who first discovered what or, more conspiratorially, to investigate whether Broca pilfered Dax's work. Nevertheless, Broca is the one who's widely credited with fully synthesizing this discovery.

with localized functions. "This opened the way," writes Oliver Sacks, "to a cerebral neurology, which made it possible, over the decades, to 'map' the human brain, ascribing specific powers—linguistic, intellectual, perceptual, etc.—to equally specific 'centers' in the brain."[10]

Broca foresaw the veritable hurricane of controversy sure to follow the presentation of his findings. In the words of Carl Sagan, he had just found "that there is a connection between the anatomy of the brain and what the brain does, an activity sometimes described as 'mind.'"[11] Broca himself wrote that this was quite "a revolution in the physiology of nervous centres," for no one had ever suggested that this most symmetrical-looking organ possessed localized, uneven distribution of higher functions, to say nothing of the fact that many people still considered the mind to be sacred and fundamentally off-limits to science.[12]

It didn't take long for Broca's peers to come up with challenges to the infant theory of cerebral localization. Broca embraced such skeptical questioning and was able to show that damage to one area of the left hemisphere would impair patients differently than damage contained specifically within this speech "center." But the more puzzling exceptions were the small number of patients with either left-hemisphere damage and no difficulties with spoken language, or the telltale inability to speak, yet only frontal lobe damage in the *right* hemisphere.[13]

Broca could only surmise that for a minority of people, localization of the speech center must be reversed between the left and right hemispheres. At one point he suggested that these people might also have their handedness reversed, i.e., that such individuals would be left-handed, but later he said these two exceptions to left-side dominance for speech weren't necessarily united. That is, they didn't have to be one and the same anomaly. Satisfied with the broader theory of hemispheric localization and the explanation it provided for speechless patients like Leborgne and Lelong, Broca was apparently ready to move on to the next scientific inquiry of the day.

A few years after the sonic boom from his findings had subsided—"How could two seemingly identical masses of grey matter of the brain be so different?"[14]—other thinkers hurried to tie up what they perceived to be the obvious, and as one current scholar puts it, "psychologically seductive" theory that Broca's research had inadvertently led them to conclude.[15]

Broca correctly observed that the faculties for speech production reside in a particular area of the left hemisphere, except for the rare instances when they don't. Because some people are an exception to the language-to-the-left rule, and because a similarly small proportion of people are left-handed, everyone and his cousin in the medical establishment figured the two must go hand in hand; lefties should have language lateralized to the right.

What's interesting about this conclusion is that few people in nineteenth-century Europe would have admitted to being left-handed. Detecting someone's left-handedness would have been difficult, with eating, writing, and other major tasks all usually carried out with the right hand. What's also interesting about this conclusion is that it's wrong. Nearly 99 percent of right-handers have language located in the left hemisphere, and about 70 percent of lefties do.[16] A different proportion, yes, but hardly the opposite; most lefty brains are like righty brains, at least as far as speech function is concerned. The rest either have language in the right hemisphere, or have it distributed more evenly between the two sides of the brain.[17]

Broca had alluded to the *disassociation* between handedness and speech housed in the right hemisphere, but he didn't press the case. Once his contemporaries drew a line linking two dots that in fact warranted no connection, the view that lefties were right-hemispheric for speech persisted for nearly 50 years. It wasn't until the early twentieth century that studies of injured World War I veterans revealed that lefties didn't necessarily have language lateralized to the right. "Broca's rule"—named for him but never asserted by him— was incorrect. As Michigan State psychology professor and left-hander Lauren Harris explains: "If people had read Broca's words more carefully," especially the part about left-handers and people with language in the right hemisphere "not being one and the same exception, then maybe we wouldn't have had a half-century of wasted efforts."[18]

Broca can't be blamed for this subsequent error. He remains an icon in the annals of lefty lore because he was the first person to finger major brain asymmetry. Lurking somewhere in the lopsided nature of our brains—not in the asymmetry of speech function to the left, but somewhere—is the mechanism that makes most people right-handed and other people left-handed.

Broca's contemporaries were wrong to assume that left-handers would necessarily be right-hemispheric dominant for language. Where they may have been on the right track, though, was the inference of *some* link between language and handedness. And they may never have gotten there without Broca.

CHAPTER 4

The Warrior

It's not like a gene thing, is it?

—*Sarah Kotora, Juniata College sophomore and recipient
of the college's scholarship for left-handed students*

After six hours in London's smoky Gatwick Airport, I
arrive late into Edinburgh and shuffle toward a Volvo
taxi. The cabbie wants to know what I'm here for, so I tell
him about my quest to find a left-handedness gene and that
the trail begins with Ferniehirst Castle in Jedburgh. He's
never heard of the castle but does launch into a speech
about why some countries have road rules for driving on the
left and others for driving on the right. The gist of his lecture ranges from stories of men escorting ladies on the left
so their right arm would be free to draw the sword from its
sheath, all the way through to Henry Ford's supposed dis-
dain for anything European and thus the switch from right-
to left-side steering in American cars.*

---

*About 30 percent of the people on Earth live in countries where driv-
ing on the left is the rule of the road (the United Kingdom, India, Japan,

The following morning, I rent a blueberry-colored Fiat and gun it for route A8. The left-side driving trips me up and, oddly enough, the left-hand gear shift. At one point, the car lurches just before a rotary, and I barely avoid a collision with two cars making their way around to the left, as their right of way permits. Finally, I settle into a rhythm, enjoying the zooming sensation when rounding the narrow curves in the countryside, passing a huge wind farm, followed by pasture after pasture with grazing sheep and cows. Before long my thoughts refocus on the mission: finding the Kerr family castle and divining firsthand what, if anything, the Kerrs might be able to teach me about the inheritability of left-handedness.

The Kerr (pronounced "car") clan supposedly arrived in Britain sometime in the eleventh century, most likely from the Stavanger area of Norway. They eventually settled into the lands of what is now southernmost Scotland, an area dotted with ancient castles and abbeys built in an age when chaos and violence were constant, thanks to the English as well as the thieving, anarchic Reivers. The name Reivers might sound gentle, reminiscent of a folk music group, but these people were ruthless. "Bandits, gangsters, what have you," says Jedburgh native and historian John Swan. "They would kill for the sake of killing."

Australia), yet how this came to be in each country, and even in certain regions of certain counties, is closely tied to the geography, industrial history, and colonial legacy of each locale, making the subject of driving laterality more complicated than it may appear. See Chris McManus, *Right Hand Left Hand: The Origins of Asymmetry in Brains, Bodies, Atoms, and Cultures* (Cambridge, Mass.: Harvard University Press, 2002), 247.

This is *Braveheart* territory, and conflict with the English defines the local history. As a Scottish territorial stronghold, Jedburgh and nearby villages like Kelso hosted countless clashes, battles, and massacres at the hands of, or delivered to, the English. In the late 1400s, Sir Thomas Kerr ordered the construction of Ferniehirst Castle, just south of what is now Jedburgh's center. Because of its location near the border, Ferniehirst was destined to be attacked and recaptured many times over. In 1523 it was sacked by the English. In 1549 the Scots, with the help of the French, retook the castle and beheaded the English garrison leader, and legend has it the Scots then used the man's head as a ball for some kind of sporting game. Nowadays in Jedburgh, the annual "Handba" game is played with a leather ball affixed with streamers, representing the hair and head of the decapitated Englishman.

Thomas Kerr is the most famous of the Kerr clan, thanks to his friendship with Mary, Queen of Scots, a relationship that improved the status of the clan considerably. But it was Thomas's son Andrew who was a natural left-hander. In an age of sword fighting in this rarely peaceful border region, Andrew found being left-handed to be an advantage for much the same reason left-handed tennis players, boxers, or fencers have an advantage. It's probably not, as much as we Southpaws would like to think, because we're inherently more gifted, except for in those cases when we are.

The lefty advantage exists because, in a world with far fewer lefties than righties, right-handed, or even left-handed, opponents have comparatively little practice facing off against left-handers. Lefty forehands are hit from that less familiar side, their stronger punches originate from that less comfortable side, and their opposing stance differs from what people are accustomed to, namely right-handed opponents. For Andrew Kerr, the matter was of far greater import than for, say, John McEnroe serving up another ace to the ad-court at Wimbledon; for Kerr, success with the sword was a matter of life and death.

Despite this tactical advantage, one early theory for the preponderance of right-handers in the human population holds that it was the dynamics of hand-to-hand battle that actually killed off most lefty progenitors.[1] Right-handers fight with a sword in the right hand and hold the shield with the left, thus better protecting the heart. Southpaws, conversely, expose the heart by fighting with the left hand and holding the shield in the right hand. Assuming an inherited role to handedness, the theory suggested that dead lefties on the battlefield meant a dearth of lefty genes, while surviving right-handers were able to pass along their genes, producing the righty majority we see today.

This easy-to-package hypothesis fails on numerous counts, most notable of which are the facts that a right-handed majority existed long before the advent of sword-and-shield warfare, and that, as any right-handed parents of left-handed children can attest, the heredity of handedness isn't so simple. In combat, it's likely the lefty advantage was more of a plus than a minus. In one of the Bible's only lefty-friendly passages, Judges 20:16 refers to Southpaw warriors aiding the Benjamites in their battle over the Israelites: "700 chosen men left-handed; every one could sling stones at an hair breadth and not miss." In fact, left-handers' fighting edge may have provided a survival advantage. Reporting in the *Proceedings of the Royal Society*, French scientists recently hypothesized that fighting advantages for left-handers in pre-historic human societies ensured reproductive success. To test the idea, they looked at the homicide rates in various societies, wondering if the Southpaw advantage might be magnified within historically more violent populations. From the results, it looks like it was, with proportions of left-handedness ranging from 3.4 percent in an especially pacifist African community in Burkina Faso to 22.6 percent in a notoriously violent culture in South America.[2] Southpaws aren't more violent, of course, but may have had a survival advantage in societies that were.

Although Ferniehirst Castle was first built by Andrew's father, Andrew probably ordered construction of the left-handed staircase, and that's what I've come to see. While most staircases in manors and castles throughout Scotland at the time were built with a clockwise spiral, Ferniehirst's main staircase spirals counterclockwise. Facing down at an ascending enemy, the lefty would be able to wield his sword in the open passage, whereas a right-handed defendant would be encumbered by the center banister, leaving him cramped and less agile, much the same way I feel when trying to wield an old-fashioned vegetable peeler.

I first heard of Ferniehirst Castle when exploring whether left-handedness is a characteristic more common in some families than others. *Kerr-handed* and *Corrie-fisted* are old-fashioned terms for a Southpaw in some northern areas of the United Kingdom. The nickname originated with the legend of the left-handed Kerr clan. One handedness expert asserts that that's all it is—a myth. Andrew's followers may have learned to fight with the sword in the left hand, but a clan of natural lefties they weren't. But the possibility of a tribe stacked with Southpaws cannot be discounted so swiftly.

———————•◆•———————

If anyone can explain the Kerr family puzzle and the heritability of handedness, it's neuropsychologist Chris McManus. On my way to Scotland I stopped into McManus's office in the Psychology Department at University College, London. McManus, a right-hander, has been researching handedness and laterality since before I was born and is the author of *Right Hand Left Hand*, an elegant and exhaustive treatise about the asymmetry of everything from hands to nucleic acids to black holes. He's also the brain behind one of the prevailing genetic models for handedness and is one of the few, maybe the only, scientist on the planet to have achieved the rather bizarre accomplishment of receiving an Aventis Prize for Science Books and the infamous Ignoble Prize from Harvard University, both in the same year. The Ignoble was for a paper about the asymmetry of testicles.

McManus has graying hair and a beard and wears an off-yellow shirt, beige slacks with almost matching socks, and white sneakers. He reminds me of the actor Richard Dreyfus, an impression solidified by his animated delivery and soprano laugh. Leading me into his office, he doesn't waste any time getting to the point. "You're left-handed because you carried a gene as an embryo that, through different biomechanisms, made the two different sides of your brain unequal."

The clarity of his statement catches me off guard. This is the first time any true authority on the subject has ever looked me in the eye and succinctly said why I'm left-handed. It's an auspicious moment, though a bit ominous if only because it means I have no choice now but to learn more about genetics.

McManus's office is decorated with brain stuff: a phrenology bust, a glass head, and a computer screensaver of a photograph taken outside the Dupuytren Museum, with Broca's bust faintly visible through the window. McManus goes on to explain that no one knows precisely what the biomechanisms are that shape our uneven brains, nor exactly how they influence handedness. "There's nothing biological in the brain that tells us if a person is left-handed or right-handed. But most researchers agree that there's something there, in the developing brain, I mean." The matter becomes more complicated and, for scholars, more titillating when a different question is asked: why are a majority of people right-handed, yet some people are left-handed?

Understanding the brain's asymmetry, for which we're indebted to people like Broca, points toward an answer to the million-dollar question, but it doesn't get us all the way there. What Broca's work did do was push beyond earlier superstitious speculation about devil curses or witchery, such as the view held by Dr. Samuel Johnson, who wrote in 1755 that "to enter the house with the skir or left foot foremost brings down evil on the inmates."[3] But if left-hemisphere damage results in speech impairment whereas right-hemisphere damage doesn't, and if damage to one side of the brain results in opposite-side paralysis, it seems reasonable to assume, as Broca did, that the roots of hand dominance also rest somewhere within our brains.

Yet that notion didn't stop generations of thinkers from postulating that handedness was determined by cultural influences. In that sense, left-handed people were still the product of some form of improper or unusual upbringing. Plato put forth one of the more famous theories when he speculated that left-handedness was "due to the folly of nurses and mothers" who failed to imprint on infants and children the cultural M.O. of the right hand's upper hand.[4]

In many ways, the debate over the origins of handedness, not only in the past but continuing today, is a classic example of nature versus nurture. Culture and the environment have undeniable effects on handedness, hence the countless stories of people being forced to write with the right hand in elementary school, swing a bat from the left side of the plate, or use chopsticks with the right hand. But does culture cause handedness?

For much of the twentieth century, as the science of neurology burgeoned and asymmetry of brain function was brought into the limelight, the prevailing theory about the causes of left-handedness shifted from one of influence on the infant to influence on the fetus. Perhaps, so the argument goes, atypical conditions in the womb effectively swap left and right (or vice versa) for at least some functions within the brain, turning a small percentage of people into Southpaws. A corollary to this idea is that some form of damage to the brain during labor causes a similar impact, somehow catalyzing a shift in hand preference from the right to the left.

To be fair to the language of science, left-handedness *is* an abnormality in the sense of a deviation from the norm, but it is not, by default, a deviation in the direction of a lesser-quality end product. A Porsche in a garage full of minivans is an abnormality too. Still, all the dire-sounding stuff about brain damage could lead, and certainly has led, some people to the faulty conclusion that lefties are, well, faulty. Even though these theories have been disputed and have lost much of their luster over the years, it's doubtful anyone would have arrived at the current paradigm for explaining handedness without the past work of others, no matter how incorrect or lefty-loathsome they may appear in hindsight. That history makes them worth a quick review.

In the 1970s and early 1980s, Harvard University neurologist Norman Geschwind put forth a theory, a favorite for many years and one that still finds pockets of support, that high levels of testosterone in the womb somehow trigger a minor change in brain organization and structure and a shift away from right-handedness. Because slightly more men than women are left-handed, the testosterone link might account for this gender difference. Geschwind and others also speculated that testosterone weakens the immune system, which helped to explain popular data at the time suggesting left-handers were more susceptible to various immune disorders. McManus concisely eviscerates this idea, however, in a section of his book titled "Vulgar Errors": "By 1994, Phil Bryden and I had unearthed eighty-nine different studies, carried out by twenty-five teams of researchers, and involving over 21,000 patients with immune disorders and 34,000 controls. Overall the results were pretty clear. Left-handers showed no systematic tendency to suffer from disorders of the immune system."[5]

When I'm feeling particularly macho, I get a little sad facing up to the fact that Geschwind's testosterone theory is probably incorrect. Geschwind is known as a laterality pioneer for accomplishments such as uncovering certain structural differences between the left and right hemispheres of the brain, but with this particular theory, he apparently missed the mark.

Another theory once suggested that orientation in the womb stimulates the fetus's sense of stability, and handedness results from whether the fetus uses the left or right hand for balance, freeing the other hand, usually the right, to move, explore, and eventually develop into the dominant one.[6] Yet another idea was that handedness is related to the season when people are born, with more left-handers born in late spring or early summer.[7] (I'm June 28, if you must know.)

Swedish scientists investigating possible adverse effects of ultrasounds on fetuses accidentally found an association between left-handedness in boys and ultrasound.[8] Not that left-handedness is an adverse effect, says Helle Kieler, an epidemiologist at the Karolinska Institute in Stockholm. But at least four studies, she adds, indicate that the chance of a boy being left-handed increases with ultrasound exposure. In Kieler's view, "left-handedness is probably genetic," but external factors such as ultrasound might also cause a shift in handedness for some individuals.[9]

To glimpse how wildly varied theories about the causes of handedness remain to this day, during one week of research, I bumped into a 2004 paper looking at the genetics versus birth stress question. After hunting for a connection between birth stresses and handedness, the researchers concluded that there simply wasn't one—a vote for the genetics argument, also known as the you're-just-born-that-way hypothesis.[10] A few days later I found another 2004 study demonstrating that the prevalence of handedness in one direction likely results from social selection pressures and not genetics—a vote for the nurture argument.[11]

An essential problem with environment-based theories—aside from the absence of strong data that can withstand the test of replication—is getting any of them to firmly gel with what we know about handedness running in families. In the 1870s, right-hander Charles Darwin had a more than minor hunch that handedness was inherited after observing that his son William was a Southpaw, as were the boy's grandfather, mother, and brother.[12] Though not a clear-cut genetic trait that "breeds true" like hemophilia, for example, handedness does run in families; it just doesn't run in a straight line.*

The probability for couples having left-handed children, according to work McManus has done synthesizing decades of surveys and studies, looks something like this: two right-handed parents have a 9.5 percent chance of having a left-handed child; one right- and one left-handed parent have a 19.5 percent chance of being blessed with a Southpaw; and two left-handed parents—a dream team of sinistral procreation—have a 26.1 percent chance of having a left-handed child.[13] Because handedness doesn't breed true, the legend of an entirely left-handed Kerr clan is a myth. But

---

*As this manuscript neared completion, the whole notion of breeding true and the certainty of genetic inheritance was called into question after scientists at Purdue University found certain plants refused to inherit a mutant gene from their parents. Whether this find could ever relate to handedness specifically I haven't a clue, but it so shook the foundation of genetics that it's worth this brief aside.

two lefty parents *are* more likely to have left-handed children, which means it's possible that, in an age of comparatively insular communities (read: more inbreeding), the Kerrs did, at one time, have an unusually high percentage of Southpaws, or just enough to kick-start a legend.

What's the deal with these seemingly bizarre percentages? Why, as one scholar put it, is the inheritance of lopsidedness so lopsided?[14] The key to heredity patterns was first uncovered by an English researcher named Marian Annett. In 1972, Annett, who doesn't take lightly to puppet jokes, published a paper titled, "The Distribution of Manual Asymmetry," which, although of little notice at the time, would later serve as the foundation for one of the most widely accepted explanations of human handedness. She called it the Right Shift Theory, and she later expanded it in a 1985 volume of the same name. Annett argues that whereas human handedness is comparable to the left- or right-side preferences exhibited by other creatures with hands, paws, feet, or what have you, the approximate 90 percent predominance of right-handedness in the human population sets us apart. All other animals have a 50–50 split between righties and lefties. According to Annett's model, handedness in nature rests on a continuum, ranging from strong left, through mixed, and then to strong right-handedness. But for humanity the *distribution* of preference and performance is dramatically shifted to the right.

Human bias to the right, Annett explains, was triggered by a shift to the left hemisphere of the brain for certain cognitive functions, most likely speech. "Speech is a very tricky thing that only humans have evolved," Annett told me by phone from her home near Leicester. She believes that the change toward further brain asymmetry marks the speciation event leading to modern humans' present, kick-ass brain capacity, and that a side effect of this change was the majorityization, so to speak, of right-handedness, coupled with an "incidental weakening of the left hand."[15] That momentous shift was caused by a gene.[16] Since Darwin, scores of scientists have suspected that handedness is inherited, but Annett's Right Shift Theory marks the first time anyone has suggested how the gene responsible for handedness might operate.

In many ways, the genes-versus-environment dichotomy is a misleading one because so often the two work hand in hand. Say, for instance, a gene or genes instructs for a certain amount of testosterone in the womb. If the level of that hormone varies and somehow influences the development of the fetus, should traits affected by the level of testosterone be dubbed genetic or environmental? One could argue that the biochemical conditions in the womb—the fetus's surroundings—qualify as environmental factors, but those conditions are shaped by genetic instructions. Yet within the DNA of every cell of that newborn baby, there will be no information specific to the child's conditions in the womb. Can we call that a genetic trait?

Luckily, Annett's theory supposes a less ambivalent role for a gene, or possibly a few genes. Inside the nuclei of nearly every cell in the body are left-twisting bundles of DNA that either do or do not contain what Annett has dubbed the "Right Shift factor." Still, to say something is genetic does not necessarily mean there's a particular gene that does or doesn't result in that trait. If only it were that easy: someone could just scroll through a person's genetic code, find a gene coding for left- or right-handedness, and we could be on our way.

Genetics isn't as linear as we'd like to think. Traits can result from single genes, various combinations or committees of genes, genes that change the probability of other genes switching on or off, or genes that change the biochemistry of a developing organism in some profoundly subtle way that science can't yet detect. Having said that, within modern-day science writing it's hip to identify a trait, disease, or even a behavior as having a genetic origin. This is for good reason. The enterprise of understanding the influence of genes on how we are made, the diseases we get, and—to a degree—who we are has grown at a mind-blowing pace in recent decades, especially with the mapping of the human genome. "For the human genome is nothing less than the instructions for how to build and run a human body," writes Matt Ridley in the opener to *Genome*.[17]

At the same time, the complexity of the human cookbook—only a tiny fraction of its meaning has been deciphered, after all—is a reminder of the predominantly still-unknown manner in which genes operate, and the puzzle of handedness is a good example. The genome has been licked, yet nobody thus far can take a characteristic as seemingly simple as hand preference and point to the exact line in the Instruction Book of Human that codes for this particular aspect of us. "The amount that we know with confidence about human handedness is so pitiful it's almost shocking," Richard Palmer of the University of Alberta recently told *TheScientist.com*.[18]

Without a neon billboard lighting a path to the appropriate gene on the genome, researchers are forced to speculate, gathering evidence and then working backward to support or refute theories about hypothetical genes. That's what Annett and McManus have done. In describing the gene in question, Annett argues that it confers bias to the right. That is, take an ordinary bell curve with a dotted line down the middle, and slide the entire bell to the right. Instead of two equally sized populations on each side of that dotted line, most of the population now sits to the right. Presto: shifted distribution.

Those who carry the right shift gene in its active or dominant form have handedness bias shifted to the right.[19] The kicker is that those who don't carry it or who carry the inactive (recessive) version are not automatically destined to be left-handed; again, if only it were that easy. In Annett's view, there may be a gene for right-handedness, but not for left-handedness. Instead, non-right-handers exist because they either lack the right shift gene and have randomly determined hand preference just like other animals, *or* their starting point on the handedness continuum is set so far to the left that even after the shift to the right, they still land on the left side of the dotted line. These people, according to Annett, are left-handed.

In a 2002 book following up on her original work, Annett offers a helpful illustration of this biased probability based on loaded dice:

Suppose that left-handedness depended on the throw of a die, the numbers 1–3 meaning "left" and the numbers 4–6 meaning "right." There would be equal chances for left and right, three of each, analogous to our primate cousins [chimpanzees]. Suppose now that two points were added to every outcome. The number on the die would range from 3 to 8. Only one number would give left-handedness (number 3) but there would be five chances for right-handedness (number 4–8).

Think of the right shift gene as a device in a Vegas casino that rigs results by adding two points onto the roll of the die. This weighted result, Annett purports, gives humanity a nearly 90 percent righty majority. The theory offers a viable explanation for the proportion of left- and right-handers we see in society, about 10 percent, maybe as high as 12.5 percent.

Another valuable way to think about this chance-influencing gene is with the help of identical twins. By definition, identical twins have exactly the same genes, and if there were a gene that simply conferred left- or right-handedness, we could safely assume that one twin would always have the same hand preference as the other twin. Yet the best estimates suggest that somewhere between 10 and 20 percent of identical twin pairs have different hand preferences. Years ago, these discordant identical twins were spotlighted as crucial evidence to undercut genetic explanations for handedness and to promote theories based on cultural and environmental influences.

McManus has twin daughters himself and was an obsessive observer of their emerging handedness: "For something to be genetic," he writes, "it is not the case that identical twins have to be the same in every way with any difference necessarily implying an environmental influence."[20] The chance element "applies separately to each twin, as if each twin separately tossed a coin."[21] Even though I'm skimming over some trickier statistics and genetics here, the key is that data about handedness in families, even among identical twins, fit the prevailing genetic models. Interestingly, twins are more likely to be left-handed, although no one is exactly sure why that's the case.

Whether or not the Right Shift Theory proves to be correct, Annett's groundbreaking insights were threefold: the idea of a handedness continuum; the chance-based gene predicting not individual handedness but shifted population distribution; and finally the suggestion that people are not left-handed or right-handed, but right-handed or non-right-handed.

But is that all Southpaws are—non-righties? What would Andrew Kerr say to that?

———•◆•———

When I pull up to Ferniehirst just before 11:00 A.M., the rain is off and on, and Ferniehirst warden Duncan Woods is standing outside to greet me. With short-cropped, graying hair in a widow's peak, Woods chuckles when I show him the plastic broadsword and scabbard I picked up in a London toy store. "Yur knut gonna do mooch damidge wit dat der," he says, taking the sword in his hand. Woods, I'm happy to learn, is a Southpaw.

The castle is smaller than I envisioned, yet absurdly picturesque. It stands proudly near the bottom of an evenly sloping hill divided into sheep pastures. The final few hundred yards before the Jed Water are taken up by a pine forest, rumored to hold caves where the Kerrs and other Scots would hide to either evade or ambush the British.

Inside the small castle museum, Woods shows me a framed family tree dating back centuries, with my hero, Andrew, down near the tree's base. We look at armor dating back to the sixteenth century, authentic swords that far outclass my plastic one, as well as examples of the Kerr family tartan of red and green, which to my eye looks like any other L. L. Bean–brand plaid.

Next, Woods swings open the heavy wooden front door to the castle. There are three steps right in front of us. The entryway is wide and although I can see that the stairs continue up to the left, I notice nothing unusual, thinking this is just the main entrance and that the real staircase I've come to see is tucked in some spooky corner somewhere. But this is it: the left-handed staircase.

For one thing, the staircase doesn't spiral. It's a staircase alright, with two 90-degree turns breaking up a total of 11 wide stone steps leading to the second floor. Woods says the main hall has been renovated a number of times, which I can tell by the magnificent wood finish and unscathed stone stairs. The walls are covered with portraits of Kerrs through the ages, as well as one of David I.

What's more of a letdown is the off-white, mechanical chairlift snaking up the outer edge of the staircase, installed a few years back to help the elderly owners of the castle make their way upstairs. Even though I'm usually sympathetic to special needs of the geriatric sort, the sense of deflation is hard to suppress, as if this rare Southpaw cultural treasure has been vandalized. But then Woods says there's one more staircase he can show me.

The next room has reddish murals on the walls depicting Kerr history through the ages, including a few battle scenes, and I easily spot the left-handers. Then Woods opens a hobbit-sized, barely rectangular door. It's the original, he says, prompting me for some reason to smell it before realizing that I don't know what I'm sniffing for—history maybe? It just smells like wood.

Beyond is a narrow, spiral staircase with white stone walls and a few black iron light fixtures subtly placed to resemble candles from back in the day. This looks more like it, the castle of my imagination, and I take out my plastic sword, handing the scabbard to Woods for him to pose as an opponent. Thankfully, he's a good sport.

At first, I can't help but imagine Andrew as an identical twin of the Dread Pirate Roberts in the comedy *The Princess Bride*. "Why are you smiling?" asks the Spanish swordsman in the midst of battle. Roberts: "Because I know something you do not know. . . . I am not left-handed." When I finally remove Cary Elwes, Billy Crystal, Andre the Giant, and the rest of the *Princess Bride* cast from my head, I get back to assessing the staircase. As Woods and I face off against each other, trying to replay what a sixteenth-century swordfight might have looked like with a lefty defending from above, we come to the conclusion that the stairwell design offers a slight advantage to a left-hander, but without authentic fencing skills, nor a sincere effort to kill each other, the degree of advantage is difficult to ascertain.

We step out into the driveway, and Woods looks at the sky. "A wee touch ah rain camin' back." With little need for the sword and scabbard, I offer them to Woods as a gift for his grandson. He says thanks and then, before parting, mentions that the black sheep just ahead are known as Hebridians, which date back to Viking times and are an extremely rare and valuable breed. "Some people come 'ere joost ta see those sheep," he says. "The older ones get right scruffy."

I think he's joking at first, but he's not. Rare, high-quality, valuable black sheep? Like left-handers, I mutter. "There ya go," he says, patting my shoulder.

As I wander down to the Jed Water before leaving, I recall something McManus had written. "Wherever one looks, on any continent, in any historical period or in any culture, right and left have their symbolic associations and always it is right that is good and left that is bad."[22] To Andrew Kerr, that wasn't the case. To Kerr and his followers, left-handedness was a prized asset: for battle, yes, but also, or so I like to think, because they knew it was special.

CHAPTER 5

Plein de Merde

I raised my right hand,
and my reflection raised its left.[1]

———

—*Haruki Murakami, "Where I'm Likely to Find It"*

That's not the way to talk to the Emperor!
You ought to follow the example of us courtiers:
let your speech be full of cunning and flattery.
Nobody talks in plain language here.[2]

———

—*Nikolai Leskov, "The Left-Handed Craftsman"*

Much of what people think about left-handedness is not shaped by neuropsychology research but rather by popular perceptions and personal experience. When plotting this investigation, I felt it would be limited if I stuck to conventional avenues of knowledge acquisition, namely academia. To delve honestly into the culture of the Southpaw, I would have to shake things up a little. That's why I enrolled in a 30-hour course called Introduction to Vedic Palmistry, taught at the Village Lac Dumouchel near Chénéville, Quebec, in the southwestern corner of the province. This handedness business, after all, is about hands and people. Because palm readers claim to know a lot about both, I thought I'd take some time to hear what they had to say.

Descending the escalator at Ottawa's sleek new airport, I spot a guy with a green piece of paper with my name on it. Francis Dejardins greets me with a soft French-accented lilt and leads me out to his black Mazda. Wedged into the plastic casing by the speedometer is an old photograph of Paramahansa Yogananda, the famous Indian yogi who founded the Self-Realization Fellowship in California.

The trip to Village Lac Dumouchel will take about 90 minutes, and as we cruise east toward the border between Ontario and Quebec, the flatness gives way to green hills with rocky flanks. We pass silos, waist-level corn, and rolls of hay dotting pastures that remind me of the drive from Edinburgh to Jedburgh. What would the lines of Andrew Kerr's palm have revealed? Do the lines of the left and right hands differ?

Dr. Ghanshyam Singh Birla founded the Birla Vedic Network 32 years ago in Montreal after immigrating from Meerut in the north of India, where he learned about Ayurvedic astrology and palmistry from his grandfather. Dejardins summarizes the school of thought this way: "The lines are always changing," he says. "And if you want to change them, they'll change even faster." He mentions a woman who once arrived at the center in a panic. She was afraid she would die in six months' time because of a palm reader's prophecy. "We don't do that here." Palmistry, he says, is to help people grow, find their potential, and improve their lives—not to tell them they're dying.

When we pull into a dirt driveway at the village, I'm relieved—impressed, actually. The place looks like a summer camp, and it turns out it is open to anyone who wants to rent a cabin by the lake, not just to palmistry and meditation enthusiasts, as I'd feared. I consider this openness to be a sign of normalcy, reducing the possibility of my being skinned, roasted, and eaten by crazed psychics. I'm not totally at ease, however, and unpacking my stuff in my room, I think back to the arrival day at camp as a kid, with that I-don't-know-anyone nervousness.

Just before dinner, I run into Sylvie Dugal, my instructor for the week. "Do you feel strong enough to begin the class tonight?" Sure, I say, wondering what I'm in for. We agree to begin after dinner, and she hands me my course book, "Introduction to Vedic Palmistry," before leaving me to dine solo. I'm the only student here.

During a lonely but delicious dinner of chick pea vegetable curry with rice, I flip through the first few pages of the booklet. "According to our approach to Palmistry, the two hands are different because each hand is attached to a different hemisphere of the brain. The right hand is attached to the left hemisphere, and the left hand is attached to the right hemisphere." Scientists might split hairs over the use of the word *attached*, but otherwise, no major foul. The text goes on to describe how the right hemisphere is the seat of emotion, intuition, and artistic ability, whereas the left hemisphere is the seat of logic and reason. Palmistry, however, takes the concept of hemispheric difference and carries it to the next level. "Since much of the basis of our Evolutionary Palmistry is based on a belief in past and future lives and each man's progress in this life, the difference in what he 'was' and what he 'is' is shown by the hemispheres of the brain. Subsequently what he 'was' or the sum total of his past life experiences is shown by the inactive hand; and what he 'is' or how the person is living in this life and what potentials he has to work with are shown by the active hand."

Closing the course book, I immediately start calculating how long it would take to walk the eight miles or so to nearby Chénéville, where I could find a bus to the airport, or at least take refuge at a local bar. A couple of nights later I actually try to get there, but the black flies are so aggressive I barely make it to the end of the village drive. I'm trapped.

Maybe this is an appropriate time for a clarification. If it isn't clear already, I have trouble imagining that the creases in either of my hands matter in any significant way. During dinner, I look down at the carefully sequestered foods on my plate and the anal-retentive tendencies revealed and think that one might successfully deduce more about me through an analysis of this plate than of the lines in my palms. I'm a skeptic, which means I don't think a mind-blowing epiphany is in the cards for me this week. But being correct is rarely as interesting as being wrong, and so I hope to have my own views challenged, perhaps even rewritten. Who knows? Maybe by the end of the Birla program, I will have powers on par with the Foretellers, telepathy-enabled beings who communicate via "mindspeak" in Ursula Le Guin's *The Left Hand of Darkness*.

After dinner, Dugal and I sit in a comfortable office lined with shelves filled with titles as varied as Dante, English poets, and psychology, as well as astrology primers and a 1971 guide to the Canadian Parliament. Incense is burning, and

Dugal pours me some water. In a thick French accent she explains how this is good water because it's magnetized. (Thick accent as in "bread" for breath, "taught" for thought, "owz" for house, and "bus" for boss.) The retreat staff, she says, put the water on magnets to "reverse its polarity," which in turn helps to eliminate toxins in the body. It tastes just like tap water.

Seated on a stool by an overhead projector aimed at a whiteboard, Dugal begins the lesson. She has long, straight, dirty blonde hair; oval glasses; and a mildly beakish nose. I can't really tell if she's 22 or 32 but am afraid to ask for fear it might look like a come-on. (I later find out she's 32.) She wears a black skirt and white top, with a "healing bracelet" on her right wrist and a braided one on her left bicep.

The first lesson consists of a number of perplexing statements. "We are all vibrations." . . . "It's also like a whirlpool." . . . "Once Saturn isn't playing his role properly, it's creating separation." . . . "Struti is the equivalent inner ear here on Earth." . . ."It's like a double lifeline, supporting the vitality, you know, so sometimes it can be a sign of somebody in your environment supporting you."

Dugal occasionally offers less confusing morsels of information, like how breathing and quiet time dedicated to relaxation are healthy habits, but only amidst a more frequent static of vague descriptions about hand morphology as manifestation of being, the houses of astrology, and most crucial of all, the indisputable reality that the lines of the hands change because free will matters and destiny is alterable. Then she introduces me to the concept of Hora, time analysis for auspicious events such as the birth of a baby or the day of a wedding. "It helps us to understand what is going on right now—what's *happening*." This tool sounds especially useful because I feel like I have no idea what's happening right now.

Next topic: "proof" of changing hands. The corresponding overhead, and many thereafter, are of clients who've had two sets of palm prints and consultation, with anywhere between a few months and ten years in between. All kinds of changes are evident. Dugal assures me that these changes are not the result of aging, nor do they come from any inconsistency with the ink or print-taking process. Later in my training, she says, I will get to see some examples of botched prints, but she never follows through on this.

Then she puts up another set of hands, and like collaborating oncologists in a hospital, we examine the images displayed on the wall. The Girdle of Venus is the name of the rounded line or cluster of lines arcing downward from the base of the middle finger, then up again toward the pinky. The Girdle is a landmark indicating artistic and/or musical talent, explains Dugal, pointing to the case study prints. "You can see that the Girdle of Venus is now all but gone as she has stopped playing piano, and she has more stress and is clearly not having as much joy in her life," as evidenced by an increase in unwanted minor lines and reduction of the Sun line. (Interestingly, nearly all the examples are of artists, writers, or musicians whose lines either improve because these people have emancipated themselves from the slavery of cubicle jobs to pursue their passions, or worsen because they've sacrificed stereotypically more creative pursuits for stable employment.)

The opportunity to delve into the issue of left versus right hands and how they impact both palmistry and personality finally arrives during my second afternoon. Free will, as evidenced by the lines of what palmists call the "active hand," accounts for only 25 percent of an individual's life path. For righties, the active hand is the right hand; for lefties, the left. The other 75 percent of who we are and what we do is defined by past experiences, habits, and characteristics of three or more previous lives; a pre-destiny of sorts that we must struggle to overcome, or at least redirect in the course of this lifetime if we want to evolve spiritually.

Although palm reading focuses on the active, dominant hand, it by no means excludes the inactive hand. The karma of our past is illuminated by the lines of the inactive hand, which is why both handprints are taken and interpreted for consultations. The left hand of right-handed people has a 75 percent impact on their lives, and vice versa for lefties.

If we know how to listen, continues Dugal, sometimes the lines will tell us that a person needs to switch his or her active hand, or at least increase the influence of the inactive hand on our lives with the help of daily exercises such as writing with the weaker hand. The luggage of karma is not necessarily filled with unwanted items. When the left-hand palm of a right-hander shows significantly better potential— potential for what, Dugal doesn't say—a shift of the hands may be advised.

When she says this, I'm reminded of the dozens of stories I've heard from naturally left-handed people who were forced to write or eat with the right hand because using the left hand was, or still is, culturally unacceptable. Suddenly back on the age-old topic of persecution based on hand preference, I ask Dugal to elaborate. She does, but the concept only gets weirder. Take the story of the left-handed musician who came in for a consultation years ago and had "bad" lines on his left hand. He was feeling insecure about stage performances. Although it's one of the most "serious" recommendations a palmist can make, Birla himself recommended the man consider at least a partial hand switch because the lines of the right hand appeared to be superior.

I ask whether the hand switch might be an unhealthy prescription, especially for people who take pride in being right- or left-handed. Dugal says that what the responsible palmist must do is explain that the joy experienced as a result of taking Birla's advice and capitalizing on all the potential currently suppressed in the inactive hand will far outweigh any present joy. Teasing, I tell her Birla better not say any such thing to me during my consultation. "You should be more open-minded," she warns.

In other cases, the lines of the two hands are too discordant, indicating that the owner of said hands has a lot to do—"a lot of files open on the table that need addressing." What palmists strive to do is harmonize the two hands, as with the two hemispheres of the brain. Sort of like yin and yang, adds Dugal, who would easily win the New Age Society award for the most frequent use of that phrase. Still, isn't switching hands for writing or other tasks a bit extreme, or possibly counterproductive?

No, she says, because it's only some switching with practice writing, not a total change. The lefty owner of one set of prints that we examine probably *wanted* to be right-handed, Dugal insists. He wanted to possess the qualities manifested in his right-hand lines in his present life, but just before he was born, it was like a sudden energy shift to the insecure past self—keep in mind the 75 percent pull of this inactive side. As a result, this man became a left-hander moments before his mother went into labor. I ask how Dugal or any-one knows about this pre-birth hand switching. Her response is unusually succinct: "Ask Ghanshyam [Birla]."

By day three I'm dying to meet this guy. He's the author of numerous books on palmistry and astrology, beloved guru to Dugal and scores of followers, an authentic Indian palmist, and the only person within 500 miles who might be able to offer any plausible insight into how palmists know what they know, how the lines of left and right hands differ, and how being left-handed matters. What will I feel in his presence? Perhaps the awe-bordering-on-worship that Dugal and Dejardins express? Will he instantly know that I think this is a sham, and if he does, wouldn't that knowledge automatically prove me incorrect? How much should I challenge him, or would it be karmically hazardous to do so?

First, though, I have to study for the daily quizzes and final exam. As my lessons proceed, I begin to show promise, especially on the short answers. *What does the comparative study of the right and left hands reveal about an individual?* My answer: "The degree to which the two hemispheres of the brain are harmonized. Also, the present self compared to the past (inactive) self that originates from the accumulated experiences and characteristics of past lives. Remember: 25 percent versus 75 percent." Dugal is impressed, and when she says "wow," I feel guilty.

That evening I go for a swim in the lake. Although the sky is the same, quiet gray as it was all afternoon, I begin to worry about lightning. Yet every time I point in a certain direction and put my head in the water to swim, thirty or forty strokes later I open my eyes to find that I'm facing opposite my intended direction. Could this be a Bermuda Triangle for disbelieving palmistry students? Finally, I turn back toward the waterfront area, head above water for much of the way, stroking until I'm completely out of breath.

My $185, one-hour consultation with Birla is scheduled for 2:00 P.M. on my last day. At breakfast I chat a little with the cook. She sees my handprints open on the table and asks if she can take a look. Holding the paper up with her left hand, she nods a few times, inspecting slowly, then says one "hmm," followed by a long "huh." I sit awkwardly with my hands in my lap, inches from shouting: "How can you possibly claim to know things about me or 'diagnose' me by looking at that piece of paper?!"

Yet at the same time, as pathetic as it sounds, I'm a little nervous about being judged in spite of the bogus criteria of that judgment. A Carl Sagan quote suddenly comes to mind: "What is more, many of these [quack] doctrines, if false, are pernicious. In simplistic popular astrology we judge people by one of twelve character types depending on their month of birth. But if the typing is false, we do an injustice to the people we are typing. We place them in previously collected pigeonholes and do not judge them for themselves, a typing familiar in sexism and racism."[3] Eventually, the cook puts the paper back down on the table, says nothing, and asks if I'd like a cup of coffee. At that moment my discomfort with this place and these people reaches what I mistakenly believe to be its zenith.

An hour later I enter Birla's office and set my glass of magnetized water on a coaster that reads: "My hands are like birds." He looks good for 63, wearing a cream-colored buttoned vest with a white long-sleeve shirt underneath, four rings, and a healing bracelet on his right wrist. He has gray wisps of hair combed straight back and a droop to the skin of his upper lip. His smile is warm and welcoming, his voice loud and distinguished.

First he examines papers prepared by Dugal containing information about me and my astrological chart. He scribbles notes and mutters a bunch of numbers in relation to my date, time, and location of birth, my wife's date of birth, the date of our marriage, and the time I arrived at the village on Monday—2:00 P.M. It would have been 1:55 P.M. if Dejardins and I hadn't stopped at a gas station outside Ottawa to pick up a snack, but I don't bother to mention such minutiae. As for the date of the marriage, it was a mere five weeks ago, which makes me an easy mark.

After eight minutes he finally speaks up, in a thick Indian accent.

"Is your wife left-handed?"

"No."

He nods and jots some more notes, muttering about vibrations and soul numbers. "1, 9, 7, 4, 3 is the body, put it all together you get 10, meaning 1 is your destiny number and your soul number. Your wife: 8 is soul number, 4 is her mind number, and 3 is her body number, 15 is the total meaning, 6 is her destiny."

I ask if not having my wife's time of birth available might skew the reading in any way.

"It would be fabulous indeed if there was her time. Because, for two reasons: according to your time of birth, she's very pretty. Beautiful. Good looking. As well as pretty independent. Very dynamic. Good body—active alert body. Body parts are beautiful too. And it is very likely that she has [extended pause] *passion*, fabulous passion to live and enjoy. Independent, happy and very comforting life. She has a deep inclination to make the best use of everything, either it is money or meager salary or anything, she would like cleanliness. Does it make sense?"

For some unclear reason, I say yes.

"So you married the right woman," he concludes, 12 minutes and 34 seconds into our session. Then he continues. "Venus is in the eighth, so you have come to the home of self learning . . . welcoming you with open arms to greet you, to help you to dive deep into your unconscious, super-conscious, subconscious, and make some use of the knowledge. Second thing: how is your spirit feeling? Your being wants to be in touch with inner self. How is your soul feeling?"

". . . So it clearly relates to an extraordinary gift God gave you to share whatever you have with the world [like this transcript], and this concern to share is primarily governed by the desire so that other people, whatever difficulties you have gone through or whatever you enjoy learning in the process, whatever you are learning you would be happy to be instrumental to bring people home—a certain awareness. . . . "

These pearls of wisdom cost me $3.10/minute (Canadian), and for the first 40 minutes of my hour are only interrupted by plugs for his books, as well as healing gemstones, tri-metal bracelets, and other spirit-enhancing goodies, all available at the village front desk. Later, a small "concern" arises because "Rahu happens to be there [on my chart, or in my house, or in my zone of the stars] and Rahu is not a planet . . . The shadowy path of Rahu, you have to watch that in the quest

you don't create problems with people . . . Rahu in the first
house of personality" apparently makes me agitated sometimes. His advice is to "ignore the ignorance of people" as
best as possible, though he warns—correctly, I might add—
that ignorant people will still annoy me. "Your consciousness can be very dynamic or dynamite at the same time."

Dugal's inability to answer questions about built-in contradictions of the palmistry curriculum, about potential for
error in the inky print-taking process, or about the flexibility of the human condition to defy what might be etched in
the lines is understandable because she's young and naïve.
But the master himself? I want to be confused, possibly impressed, maybe even moved beyond comprehension. Instead, it's worse than simply not believing. I feel used.

Near the end of the session, I finally get my chance to in-
quire about the different hands. Recalling the case of the
man whose soul wanted to be right-handed but whose active
hand somehow switched just before birth, making him a
left-hander, I ask Birla how he knows this switch occurred.

"We know that most of the time. We can see the child is
born to succeed or not."

And success is related to handedness?

"Yes! Yes, yeah. Handedness," he says, before launching
into a string of more nonsense. I don't bother asking for
clarification. Instead, and by this point really just for sport, I
ask about the superiority of left-handers.

"I would say the left hand is better because you want to
be a musician, because you want to be a writer. Because of
some inspiration-related work or some feeling-related work. I
find generally left-handed people have a streak of sensitivity,

positive sensitivity, *and* they can turn this sensitivity into productivity or into solid creativity better than right-hemisphere people [he means left-hemisphere people]."

Finally, the man is making a little sense. And if the active or dominant hand represents the present, whereas the inactive hand, in my case the right, represents three or more past lives, what does that say about handedness in previous lives? Was I right-handed in a previous life?

"Probably not," says Birla. "You know why I say that? My deduction is your left hand will not become as profoundly better, as good, as profoundly wonderful, or extremely positive in one lifetime. It takes a lot more than one lifetime to become good."

At last, there it is; solid confirmation that being a Southpaw is about more than writing with one hand or the other and is inseparable from sunny adjectives like "creative," "wonderful," and "positive." Maybe left-handedness really *is* something powerful that gets to the very spiritual core of one's being, in this life and beyond. Other faiths rely on equally intangible evidence. Why should the Sect of Southpaw be any different?

Although my session has run overtime, I'm granted one final question. I ask if Birla will give me the sniff test. Earlier in the week, I learned that people with less-than-desirable, conic-shaped palms have skin that's "sweet-smelling, without any artificially scented products," and this clue can lend insight into a person's spiritual constitution.

"No, your hand is conic inclined maybe but not really."

"Can you smell it anyway, just to make sure?"

"One finger," he says.

"Left hand? Active hand?"

"Yes."

I put out my left hand. He smells my index finger quickly, then looks at my palm.

"See, this is conic here . . . "

"Wait. Before the comments, tell me about the smell."

"There's a sweeter smell. See, look here. There is a conic pattern. There is a little conic pattern, slightly, one-quarter conic pattern. It even goes to one-sixth, one-fifth, one-tenth . . . this is very important for you to really, eh, it is an anxiety concern more. But there is smell here," he says, this time with bolstered import. Then he holds my hand again, cradling it ceremonially in both of his. Bringing it his nose, he closes his eyes and takes a deep sniff. "A sweeter smell," he says. "A fragrant one."

Before I can ask about the smell in light of my palm's spatulate dimensions and any connection to handedness, there's a knock on the door. It's time for his next consultation.

CHAPTER 6

Talking Hands

When he finally had enough brain to be
able to guess what the brain itself was doing,
Homo pronounced himself *sapiens*.[1]

———————

—Frank R. Wilson, The Hand: How Its Use
Shapes the Brain, Language, and Human Culture

The palm reader's evaluation gets me thinking about talking. Not the content of speech necessarily, but just a person's ability to talk, and talk, and talk. What I would come to realize soon after returning from Quebec is that the human capacity for speech plays an integral part in the debate about the origins of handedness.

Speech is a tricky thing, as Annett put it, and as far as anyone can tell, an exclusively human trick. In London, I'd attended a brain science lecture given by an Oxford researcher who, although using terminology that flew about six stories over my head, concluded the session by declaring: "It all comes back to Broca in the end." The asymmetry Broca spotted, together with human capacity for language, are essential parts of the handedness mystery. Most laterality experts today agree that handedness is inextricably linked to the phenomenon of the asymmetrical brain. Where the disagreements begin is whether or not the agent for lopsided hand use is the same agent that catalyzed the evolution of language-capable minds.

Asymmetrical brains are not unique to humans. On the contrary, brain duality has been shown to exist in many animals and traces far back in our vertebrate history, certainly further back than the origin of our species. Where humans may differ is "the nature of the processes that are lateralized," writes New Zealander Michael Corballis. What, precisely, is lateralized may hold the key to who we are and why we're so different from other animals, despite sharing more than 98 percent of the same genes as chimpanzees.[2] Among those processes that likely set us apart, language, and more specifically the capacity to produce and process speech, is tops.

Our evolutionary ancestors surely had lopsided brains, but they couldn't talk. At some point this population of noncommunicative or minimally communicative primates, with an equal number of lefties and righties, underwent a monumental evolutionary change, beyond the obvious loss of body hair and vine-swinging talent. Something opened the door, neurologically speaking, for language.

Annett argues that that something was the right shift gene. In her view, the effects of the gene thrust certain operations to the brain's left hemisphere, enabling the development of speech and eventually the modern human brain. This change, she asserts, marks, or is closely timed with, the branching moment at which we as a species went our separate way from our primate cousins. A byproduct of this shift was population-wide bias for right-handedness.

Famed linguist Noam Chomsky argues that the capacity for language is a signpost for humanity. Annett purports that spoken language *and* a right-handed majority together compose that signpost. But if right-handedness "serves as a marker for humanity," then where does that leave left-handers?[3]

The association between handedness and language touches on some of the most fundamental questions about evolution and the mind, and connections between hands, language, and the brain have been the subject of inquiry among some of history's greatest thinkers. Darwin guessed that bipedalism freed up our hands for other tasks, such as gathering food or creating shelter. Since then, scientists have been trying to piece together a plausible picture of the course of events that turned us into language-equipped toolmakers who not only write symphonies but also manipulate our environment and contemplate our existence like no other creatures in Earth's history.

It may be that anatomical changes to the hands themselves spurred the lopsided evolution of our brains, which *then* led to bias for one hand over the other. Arguing that increased sophistication of the human hand was pivotal in the evolution of the modern brain, neurologist Frank R. Wilson writes: "'Intelligent' hand use might [have opened] the door to an enormously augmented range of movements and the possibility of an unprecedented extension of manual activities. As a collateral event, the brain was laying the foundations of cognitive and communicative capacity."[4] Harvard psychologist Steven Pinker makes a similar case, arguing that our ancestors' intelligence may have increased "partly because they were equipped with levers of influence on the world, namely the grippers found at the end of their two arms."[5]

Carl Sagan suggests the next step, connecting increasingly complicated and uneven brain function directly to language: "It is very plausible that human thought and industry went hand in hand with the development of articulate speech, and Broca's Area may in a very real sense be one of the seats of our humanity, as well as a means for tracing our relationships with our ancestors on their way toward humanity."[6]

Other elements of human behavior and anatomy, such as the capacity for religion and the position of the larynx, are also unique traits whose respective emergences have been nominated as possible calendar pegs indicating the birth date of *homo sapiens*. Then again, one could argue that these aspects of us are intertwined with the evolution of language-capable brains. The key point is simply that language may indeed be the primary trait differentiating us from other animals, and predominant right-handedness its trusty sidekick.

Communication through language requires numerous skills and brain functions as varied as memory, sound recognition, syntax, speech production, grammar, and gesticulation. Annett and others believe cerebral dominance set to the left enabled early human brains to handle all this heavy-duty processing. Right-handedness and speech are markers for humanity not in the individual sense, but because no other primate species exhibit this bias for the right side. "But," Annett is quick to add, "that doesn't mean everyone has to be right-handed. It's the distribution that's different."

If humans are the only organisms equipped for spoken language, and a right-handed majority is a byproduct of the brain organization that makes speech possible, then it would make sense that no other population of animals has handedness skewed to the right. Some experts argue that other animals *do* have population-level bias for right-handedness, but Annett and her supporters challenge the validity of this work and assert that right-handedness, like language, is unique to humans.[7]

The idea that the emergence of language is what initially set humanity apart from other animals is both a popular and dangerous one. It's popular because we have Shakespeare and the Beastie Boys among our ranks. Other animals—without knocking the awe-inspiring intricacy of their minds, social interactions, and communications—do not, nor do they possess comparable linguistic capabilities. It's also popular because Annett's theory, though tweaked here and there, has lasted more than three decades.

Yet using speech, language, or anything really to assert human uniqueness is dangerous because it hints at the notion of human dominion over all things and, carried to its extreme, has an outright antievolution stench to it. As Corballis writes, it "may reflect an age-old desire to place humans on a pedestal above other species, closer to angels than apes."[8] If the Right Shift allowed language to emerge, "what about those who don't have the Right Shift?" asks Corballis. In his view, the chance gene for handedness is plausible, but he believes the idea of the Right Shift as a necessary condition for language needs to be euthanized.

Most efforts to find examples of human superiority have a dismal record within the history of science, virtually always doomed to be paved over by research revealing evolutionary traces, vestiges, or similar mechanisms shared between us and other critters. I don't think any of today's laterality players have an overtly "Humans Rule!" agenda, and in their respective explorations of the question of what makes us left- or right-handed they appear to be doing so in the spirit of species differentiation and not a covert religious crusade. Nevertheless, the notion of a sudden, dramatic emergence of language-capable brains and right-handedness—versus a gradual evolution of brain organization—remains a contentious one.

But what advantages were conferred on early humans by having certain processing centers set to one side of the brain or the other? Opposing thumbs and bipedal movement have their evolutionary advantages, probably truckloads of them, but where's the advantage in uneven brain operations?

It comes down to processing power. Because the brain consists of billions of neural connections in a "microarchitecture" of dazzling efficiency, for the mind, as in real estate, location is everything.[9] "Other animals—whales, songbirds, etc.—have evidence of lateralized brains too," says Annett. "To produce and listen to a complex stream of sounds, it helps to have a lateralized brain."[10] Compartmentalized organization of such brain operations as sound production and processing increases their efficiency, and compartmentalization in the brain also means asymmetry.

It would be hugely inefficient if when reading a paragraph of text aloud, the parts of the brain charged with recognizing words, understanding grammar, sending motor instructions to the vocal chords and mouth, and processing sounds were all scattered to the far corners of both sides of the brain, passing information back and forth between the hemispheres via that limited bundle of fibers, the corpus callosum. Speed matters, and a disorganized brain can hinder speed.

Following the rationale that closely knit operations in the brain make for greater efficiency, one might then ask why language landed in the left hemisphere and not in the right. Chris McManus addresses this matter by suggesting that the left hemisphere may be a slightly faster processor, but this could be a classic standoff between a chicken and an egg; it's equally possible that the asymmetry of function on the left side led to speedier performance of certain tasks in that hemisphere. Corballis suggests that as communication through gestures came to incorporate more and more accompanying sounds, "the asymmetry in the control of the vocal chords might have favored the left hemisphere and the right hand."[11] Once that favored status was established, it may have stuck during the evolution of language. However it happened, language went to the left hemisphere and at that moment, according to Annett, handedness went to the right hand.

But not for everyone. What about people with language lateralized to the right, and people with hand preference on the left? "That was the puzzle," says Annett, now 73, reflecting on the early years of the Right Shift Theory. The gene, she says, hasn't spread throughout the entire human population, nor is it necessarily destined to do so. There's nothing unusual about that; the same could be said for the gene conferring black hair color, for instance, so lefties shouldn't feel shortchanged.

Other scientists have suggested that a gene sending language to the left of the brain and handedness usually to the right hand implies some sort of defect for left-handers. Annett insists that's a misinterpretation of her model. "Chance happens to everybody! It's a toss of a penny, but some people carry a penny that has a bias on it. And some of those people tossing the penny are still left-handed." What's more, she says, because all people aren't right-handed, "there has to be some advantage to *not* having the chance gene."[12]

It's not an advantage for the individual per se but rather for the population. Many traits persist in populations not because they're critical but because evolution finds them to be harmless, conferring no noticeable advantages or disadvantages in terms of fitness in the evolutionary survival sense (i.e., success passing genes on to offspring). Still, over time, less common traits are likely to be bred into extinction. Whereas early humans who smelled like saber-toothed tiger bait would have been selected out of the population, lefties, as far as anyone can tell, have been stubbornly present in human history, suggesting Southpaws are here for a reason.

One possible evolutionary plus to left-handedness may have to do with brain organization. Left-handedness may be a sign that lefty brains are organized differently, and that could be advantageous. This leads to McManus's own explanation for left-handedness, an overarching idea he calls "the theory of random cerebral variation." According to the theory, some people carry a gene coding for additional variability of what's where within the brain.

Gathering together studies suggesting that left-handers might be more prone to such disorders as dyslexia, schizophrenia, and stuttering, as well as other reports that left-handers might show more variability with intelligence (i.e., more Mensas and more morons), McManus was able to synthesize what appeared like hopelessly scattered ideas: the left shift for speech dominance; inconclusive research about how lefties might cognitively differ from righties; and the concept of varied geography of function inside the brain.

He believes that sometime after humans evolved lopsided brains and population-wide right-handedness, a second, more recent gene emerged to spice up the brains of those who carried it, with an additional pinch of randomness. One possible outcome of inheriting this gene is left-handedness, although many right-handed people would also be carriers. But people who don't carry the gene will not be left-handed.

Every person's brain has a certain degree of anatomical uniqueness. Most of the time, extra shuffling of brain furniture has no major noticeable effect. Other times, however, it can either help or hurt.[13] In other words, dyslexia or stuttering may result from this random arrangement of function, just as easily as Bill Clinton's gift for gab or da Vinci's visual-spatial genius may have resulted from it. The essence of randomness is that its influence, in this case on the brain, is unpredictable. It could be beneficial or compromising.

From an evolutionary standpoint it can be good to differ, and that difference alone could account for the persistence of this extra brain randomization and left-handedness through human history. It can be disadvantageous to differ too much, but overall, "the benefits have to outweigh the negatives, or it [left-handedness] would have faded as a trait long ago," says McManus. "It is a happy accident, not a situation in which something was damaged."[14]

"The real question is why everyone wants left-handers to be defective," McManus told *Discover* magazine in 2002, suggesting that other models require additional explanation to account for Southpaws, such as brain damage at birth or fetuses drunk on testosterone. Few people in the business of laterality research aside from McManus, however, are troubled by this parenthetical lefty otherness. A theory elegantly describing the right-handed majority, after all, is correct the majority of the time.

How McManus's hypothetical gene is passed through the population is similar to Annett's roll of the rigged die, allowing McManus's theory to also groove with existing data on left-handedness running in families.[15] But whereas Annett argues that left brain dominance for speech led to right-handedness and "incidental weakening of the left hand," McManus has bet on an additional gene that, through the roll of a different set of dice, gives carriers slightly more randomized brain organization. Some of those carriers are Southpaws.[16] Then again, not everyone buys McManus's idea of an additional gene conferring left-handedness. "I find it un-parsimonious and implausible," says Corballis.[17] But for now, McManus is sticking with his maverick hypothesis.

One attractive aspect of McManus's model is that lefties and righties are practically the same, and indeed many righties have the same extra bit of brain reshuffling and could have turned out to be lefties had the toss of the die produced a different result. It's a rather egalitarian concept compared with the idea that most of the human population has shifted over to the right, except for the handful that hasn't, even though Annett insists there's no deficit associated with this minority population. In general terms, both McManus's and Annett's theories lean heavily on the idea that a genetic signal either confers bias to one side or it doesn't, and in that sense it's safe to say, as Corballis asserts, that "most theorists have indeed accepted that human handedness is biological rather than cultural."[18]

Whether anyone will ever find the handedness gene or genes is hard to know. Another Englishman, Timothy Crow at Oxford, claims to have found the handedness gene in a region of the X and Y chromosomes. But because another scientist told me anonymously that this is "nonsense," I'm sticking with the doubters for now.

Meanwhile, National Cancer Institute researcher Amar Klar has put forth evidence correlating handedness with the direction of the hurricane-like hair whorl atop the scalp. Righties apparently show a counterclockwise rotation to the whorl, whereas lefties and mixed-handers show a "random mixture of clockwise and counterclockwise swirling patterns," application of high-octane hair gel notwithstanding. Because hair whorl is a trait dictated entirely by nature, Klar uses this finding to put to rest any nurture arguments for the origins of handedness. Find the hair whorl gene, he insists, and you will have found the handedness gene as well.[19]

In the bathroom mirror of my room at London's Copthorne Tara Hotel, I try to see if my hair has a clear whorl or an unclear "swirling pattern," and then figure out if said whorl looks like a hurricane in the northern or southern hemisphere. This task is tricky because I'm looking at a reflection of the back of my head, not to mention my established ineptitude orienting with mirrors (remember the Japanese barbershop). The verdict: with my hair brushed forward like one of the Beatles, the back cowlick appears to be a clockwise whorl, though it just as easily could be a symmetrical, splash-like pattern. A few weeks later, a barber confirms for me that it whorls clockwise.

Back in McManus's office, I ask what he thinks about the prospects of someday locating the Southpaw gene. He isn't optimistic, mentioning one group that's trying to look for it but adding that they likely won't find anything because they're studying left-handers exclusively. That's a doomed method, he says, because many right-handed people would also carry the chance gene. Plus, funding for this sort of pursuit is scarce, meaning few or no targeted searches for the gene.

If the gene is discovered, it will happen one of three ways. The first is serendipitously. In genetics, serendipitous discoveries happen when researchers, studying one topic, be it eye color, heart disease, or hay fever, accidentally stumble upon something completely different. In their findings, if a group of subjects are distinguished because they all, out of pure luck, happen to be left-handers too, the scientists would know they'd hit a genetic link between two traits that before were as unrelated as chalk and cheese. If the hair whorl idea turns out to be correct—and if Klar or someone else can find the gene for hair whorl—that discovery would be precisely this kind of linkage, although in this case someone hypothesized the gene's existence beforehand. Truly serendipitous finds are gifts from the heavens for geneticists, and they're also very rare.

The second possibility is that scientists become more adept at understanding the determinants of asymmetry, from cells to the heart's placement a little to the left and on up the chain of development to localization of function in the brain and ultimately to hand preference. These are the underlying biomechanisms that make people, brains, and—somehow—hand use asymmetrical.

The final way to find the gene or genes responsible for handedness might be with the help of the decoded chimpanzee genome. Comparing the DNA of humans and chimps, scientists should be able to locate the Right Shift chance gene and/or the gene conferring random cerebral variation that humans have and that chimps don't.

That's assuming people like Annett and McManus are correct in saying chimps don't have population bias toward right-handedness. Both of their theories are built on this supposition. McManus clearly states that humans recently incorporated the gene for random cerebral variation, well after the separation of human and chimp lineages. "If I'm correct and chimps do not have [population bias for] right-handedness, then there's going to be a difference in the chimpanzee genetic sequence," and that difference should be discernible. "If Hopkins is right, however, then there won't be."[20]

"Hopkins" is Bill Hopkins, a chimpanzee expert at the Yerkes Primate Research Center in Atlanta and the next name on my list.

CHAPTER 7

Pitching Chimps

All the same I think I'd better warn you
not to try any monkey business with me . . . [1]

—Nikolai Leskov, "The Left-Handed Craftsman"

"Look at that!" says Bill Hopkins, nudging my elbow. "Watch how she stands and hits the coconut on the wall." Staring down from the metal yellow perch above the fenced enclosure, we watch a chimpanzee named Liza open a coconut by whacking it against a concrete wall with her right hand. A technician notes the number of hits: one, then three, then three again. "Isn't that beautiful?" asks Hopkins.

We're watching a group of twenty chimpanzees at the field station of the Yerkes Regional Primate Research Center at Emory University. A few of the animals take sticks from the woodchip floor of the compound and chew them into probing tools that they then try, unsuccessfully, to poke through the nubs of the coconuts to access the milk inside. "Borie, it's not a dipping task," Hopkins calls down to one of the older females. Sometimes the chimps use their left hand, sometimes their right, and sometimes they hold the stick in their mouths. On this day, Borie, Kathy, Socrates, and Rhett are among the chimps that attempt this method, before wising up to the fact that hitting the nut against concrete will serve them better.

"Socrates is probably the most left-handed of the ones here," says technician Jamie Russell. "And he's also the alpha male, so there you go," she jokes. After a while, Socrates takes the coconut that he'd been coveting and walks over to a cylindrical piece of concrete the size of a trash barrel. He climbs on top and begins banging the coconut, first with his left, then with his right arm. Meanwhile, Hopkins and his team count and note left versus right hands whenever the chimps whack, poke, climb, cradle, feed, or gesture, the latter usually directed up toward us as a plea for more food.

"Watch how Missy moves her right index finger when you're about to throw her something," says Hopkins. I see Missy's pensive face staring back at me, her right arm stretched skyward and her long finger wiggling up and down. A few minutes later, we watch another chimp grooming her thick fur, and Hopkins again directs my attention to the delicate movements, this time of the animal's right thumb, which looks as if she were scratching away the silvery coating of a lottery ticket.

Although the air is chilly and the sprawling facility smells of woodchips and manure, I could sit on this perch for hours, riveted. Observing a group of chimpanzees, or even just one chimp staring upward and begging for a coconut, is a profound experience. I won't profess to any Jane Goodall impulse to spend the next few years of my life living among them, mimicking their snorts and chest-pounding. But watching them manipulate tools, throw tantrums, groom one another, and clap their hands stirs a feeling that I'm not just looking at hairy animals that happen to resemble people, but seeing straight into the past.

As far as Southpaws are concerned, whether chimpanzees are a link to *our* past is why I'm here. Prevailing wisdom about the origins of handedness runs into some turbulence, if not an all-out tailspin, as a result of right-hander Bill Hopkins's psychobiology work with primates. Hopkins's findings don't necessarily make answers easier; if anything, the picture only gets blurrier from here. But they're too important and too interesting to ignore.

Standing about 5′8″, Hopkins has widely set blue eyes, wears a diamond stud in his left ear, and has the disposition of a 1970s rocker. "I'm not as much of a theorist as I am a tester of theories," he says, sipping coffee at the Living Links offices, an adjunct facility to the Yerkes operation. The center is surrounded by imposing, barbed-wire-topped fences— not to keep the animals in, one employee tells me, but to keep misguided animal-rights protesters out.

The thrust of Hopkins's work suggests that chimps are like humans. That alone is hardly a novel claim, considering chimps are our closest living relatives. Where things start to get groovy is that Hopkins has found that chimps, with regard to handedness, resemble humans more than other primates.

Then again, handedness in our closest living relatives isn't much of a newsflash either. Many animals show lateral preferences, programming, physiology, or all of the above. Individual elephants, for example, appear to prefer swinging the trunk upward on one side more than the other, and housecats, mice, and rats show paw preferences for different tasks. When it comes to arms, paws, or claws, scientists—at least before Hopkins and a few other dissenters arrived on the scene—generally agreed that most animals, including *all* nonhuman primates, have randomly determined lateral preference. In other words, the only determinant of left or right preference in the nonhuman animal kingdom is chance, so individual creatures are just as likely to be lefty as to be righty. Humans, or so everyone thought, are the exception, with our skewed—some might say screwed up—9:1 ratio of righties to lefties.

Although asymmetrical limb preference is randomly determined in most animals, one exception for population-level sidedness comes from parrots.[2] The same 9:1 ratio appears in most species of parrot, except the bias is reversed, with a 90 percent majority favoring the left foot for picking things up. No one is sure why this is the case, and the finding strikes me as one of those curious anomalies, hanging around for someone to decode. Maybe it will lend insight to the wider brain- and body-sidedness puzzle, or maybe it will just turn out to be a tidbit for the files of parrot foot trivia.

Hopkins's chimps don't fit the predicted 50–50 split either. For nearly fifteen years, he has been observing chimps' behavior, closely tracking their handedness preferences for tasks as varied as scooping honey from plastic tubes, cradling infants, cracking open coconuts, and (my favorite) throwing shit. What he's found is a population-level bias for the right hand. It's not always present for all tasks, nor is it a 9:1 ratio as it is for humans. But it's there. Hopkins estimates that about 70 percent of Yerkes chimps are right-handed. The other 30 percent could loosely be called lefties.

This finding is contentious and, though it's tough to imagine these academic types getting truly ticked off, their debates get rather heated. Some researchers have emphatically declared that chimpanzees don't and can't have population-level right-handedness, in essence discounting in a single sentence most of Hopkins's research. "The best I can say is that he's got a curious sample," says Annett, suggesting that the Yerkes bunch isn't representative of chimpanzees in the wild. Other experts also suspect that more frequent right-hand preference may be restricted to chimpanzees in captivity. Various creatures certainly have brain asymmetry like humans, but consistent right-handedness, they assert, is unique to humans.[3]

So how does Hopkins make his case? After all, you can't just ask a group of chimps who's a lefty and who's a righty, nor present them with questionnaires and a bunch of No. 2 pencils. Then again, as Hopkins likes to point out, much of the "noise" of cultural factors is canceled out when doing studies based solely on observation. Ask a person what hand he uses to brush his teeth, and he might have three different answers, two of them with tandem caveats, another one with a dozen qualifiers, and by the way did I tell you about my possibly left-handed nephew? But with chimps, you can watch and count how many times and with what hand the animals hit the coconut against the wall, and then do some statistical analysis, publish your work, and wait for the mud-slinging or praise-singing to begin.

One of the more recent and striking areas of inquiry has to do with throwing. During my visit to Atlanta, we watch as Socrates flicks dirt and woodchips toward one of the ranking females, his erect organ indicating interest in something other than Tara's coconut. But Tara shows no reciprocal interest. A few minutes later, perched atop one of the metal jungle gyms in the enclosure, she throws a stick in an over-the-shoulder motion down toward two of the other chimps seated by a barrel. The trajectory is a smooth, arcing rainbow, and the stick lands about two feet from the (presumed) intended target.

Chimpanzees will throw sticks, bits of food, and dirt, but most often shit, usually at their friendly neighborhood primatologists. The animals throw to get a researcher's attention, to pester for food, to declare machismo, and probably a whole host of other reasons. "If they're going to throw at me, I figure I'm going to get some data out of it," says Hopkins, as only a true scientist could. After tracking lateral preferences for throwing, Hopkins found that out of 91 chimps at Yerkes, all but two of them show strong bias for overhand throwing with the right hand.

When the animals do an underhanded hurl, like Socrates's earlier flicking, less sophisticated coordination is required, as compared to launching an overhand projectile. For the underhand action, Hopkins has found little difference in terms of right- or left-arm preference. Why is it that when the chimps make upright, pitcher-like throws, all but two of them consistently throw with the right arm? No other animal on the planet besides humans performs this kind of motion, nor are any other creatures, at least according to the Right Shift Theory, supposed to have overall bias for right-handedness.

Hopkins has also found that when the animals move about the enclosure and execute the underhand hurl *at the same time* that they're moving, those throws are usually done with the *left* hand. The hypothesis is that the preferred right hand is prioritized for assisting with locomotion. Remember, in spite of the tendency to personify Liza, Rhett, and the rest of the *Gone with the Wind* cast, these knuckle-walking animals are usually moving around on three or four limbs.

This right-side preference or prioritizing among chimps, which has since been documented elsewhere besides Yerkes, leads to rather provocative, although preliminary, conclusions. For food-related tasks like digging honey out of a plastic tube or cracking open coconuts, the chimps demonstrate a relatively even distribution of left/right preference (i.e., no right shift in handedness). The same is true for underhand, less dexterity-dependent shit-hurling. But for more precise, over-shoulder throwing, chimps are more like humans; most are right-handed.

Hopkins makes sense of these discoveries by distinguishing between tasks for obtaining food that, although not necessarily simple, require less prerequisite brain power than tool-manipulation tasks for interaction or communication. Throwing, after all, is a form of tool use in the sense that it utilizes an object for a specific objective and requires careful movement.[4] University of Washington neurobiologist William Calvin writes that accurate throwing is "reminiscent of syntax." It is a kind of structured planning of muscle coordination with an understanding of space, force, and time far more advanced in terms of brain power than, for instance, what was required for earlier primates to smash two rocks together, hoping the result would produce a useful shard.

Lucy, the earliest known direct human ancestor, was found in eastern Africa and is estimated to have lived some 3.2 million years ago. As described by neuroscientist Frank R. Wilson, the shape of her hand bones indicate that she was equipped to pound stones, which probably wasn't a first in primate history. It's also apparent that she was able to throw with accuracy and speed. "Lucy, in other words, might have been at home on a pitcher's mound."[5]

If the motivation for throwing relates to some kind of interaction between the animals or between an individual chimp and a researcher, could it be that handedness in chimps is manifest only for this communication-type movement of the limbs but not for more primal movements like accessing and eating food? If so, perhaps this demonstration of right bias is a window into the same process of asymmetry— of brain and hand—evident in humans. Overhand throwing requires significant cerebral *umph*, which Hopkins calls "neuro-physiological demands." Could this type of throwing be a precursor to the modern human mind and "higher aspects of consciousness," especially language, that set us apart from the rest of the animal kingdom?[6] Maybe the brain wiring for throwing was just one of many such precursors and, as far as handedness goes, an essential one at that.

Yet Michael Corballis refutes the role of throwing as a key determinant in the evolution of handedness because if one-armed throwing were indeed so essential to our evolutionary story, humans would have obvious structural asymmetry between the two arms. If the very survival of *Homo sapiens* hinged on the throwing accuracy of one arm over the other, we'd have one clearly souped-up arm like lobsters do, not two symmetrical ones.[7] But what if throwing was critical to human evolutionary history, yet instead of an overtly structural adaptation, ours was one of heightened coordination?

———•◆•———

To get a better idea of this coordination stuff, I drop in on Robert Sainburg at Pennsylvania State University's Movement Neuroscience Laboratory, tucked into a building shared with a gymnasium and locker rooms. Within minutes Sainburg has his hands on my arm for a demonstration. "Just relax your muscles," he says, sounding more like a personal trainer than a scientist. With one hand under my upper arm and one on my shoulder, he pulls quickly, causing my forearm and wrist to whip outward like a string puppet. He does this a few more times, making my arm feel rubbery and out of control.

When you reach out to grab, pick, press, or push things, your forearm, explains Sainburg, doesn't whip around wildly because even though your shoulders generate plenty of power for the whole arm to move and the forearm to swing, your bicep intercedes to check the powerful motion of the forearm so that the hand stops precisely at the edge of the counter, just as an egg, for instance, is about to roll off and splatter on the floor. This kind of dissecting analysis of coordination is what Sainburg's research is all about.

Coordination. How often we curse the gods for not having more of it when maybe we should be thanking them for how much we have. To guys like Sainburg, coordination doesn't just mean the ability to juggle tangerines. "It's the ability to match muscle forces with biomechanical factors in order to achieve a desired movement." That ability is the reason we can retrieve a wineglass from the back of the cupboard without knocking over all the neighboring glasses and dishes.

How is it that muscles "know" to check the forearm from swinging far past a target? The quick answer is anticipation. The more relevant answer for this conversation is that the brain models movement. This mapping of upcoming forces is the coordination we take for granted a million times a day—lifting a frying pan, driving a car, throwing a ball.

But as anyone can tell you, there's a clear and present difference in the coordination level of the dominant versus the nondominant hand, and it's this disparity that truly distinguishes lefties from righties in everyday life. Sainburg has been exploring this difference, and his emphasis on movement has led to clever new ideas about the role of each hand and the origins of handedness. "All these theories are driven by the assumption of an association between handedness and language or cognition," that handedness somehow spun off from or fell out of the evolutionary process of left brain control of speech. "That's weird to me. I think it has to do with motor coordination."[8]

In looking at the intricate brain-body communication required for movements like throwing a spear, Sainburg suggests evolutionary pressure for increased coordination resulted in, or selected for, brains better equipped to carry out more sophisticated movement. "Motor coordination is such a prominent feature of adaptive behavior that it undoubtedly played a large role in survival during the early days of our species' evolution."[9] It's a similar idea to that of brain organization, or reorganization, enabling the development of such functions as language, but the *selective pressure* to maximize brain power in this case may not have been cognition but coordination. Did brain lopsidedness for motor function precede brain lopsidedness for cognitive function?

Hopkins's chimps, throwing but unable to talk, make a compelling case for the argument that brains first became rigged for coordination, followed by further changes that led to language. "The forces that led chimpanzees to lateralize to a degree—might those same forces have acted on us and made us lateralize to a more exquisite degree?" asks Sainburg. Perhaps when coordination demands shaped the brain, that's when handedness first happened. When language demands came along and shaped the brain a little more, handedness happened a little more too, which would explain why humans are even more lopsided in their right-handedness than chimps.

If Hopkins's chimps prove to have some population-level shift to right-handedness, that finding forces an overhaul of theories like Annett's that assume bias for right-handedness is a uniquely human phenomenon. The Right Shift Theory fits so well, or perhaps I should say is so easily coupled, with speech because if speech and a righty majority are both exclusively human traits, then it's reasonable to suspect they spun off of the same evolutionary agent for change. But if Hopkins is correct and chimp populations also show right-bias, whatever mechanism it was that caused mostly right-handedness— let's assume a gene—was already onstage in the great play of primate evolution, acting in a scene prior to the one in which early humans first began to communicate with speech. Should that be the case, then the Right Shift Theory is in deep chimp shit. And if theories for the causes of right-handedness get shaky, decent answers about the causes of left-handedness are more of a long shot than ever.

Over a dinner of ribs and beer at his home in State College, Sainburg shares another tantalizing aspect of his research: a paradigm bunker-busting notion that there may be no such thing as dominant and nondominant limbs. Recall

Corballis's straightforward definition of right-handedness from Chapter 2: "The right hand dominates in tasks involving both hands, such as unscrewing a jar." But according to Sainburg's research, each hemisphere-limb duo has different specializations, and the system controlling the nondominant limb appears to be superior at handling certain functions. In other words, the right hand of a right-hander may be charged with unscrewing the lid, but that person's left hand is engineered to steady the jar.

Whereas laterality research tends to lean heavily on field observation, Sainburg employs controlled experiments, including a custom-built virtual reality setup designed to examine coordination. Test subjects sit at a table and then use one arm to direct a cursor to an illuminated target. The cursor reflects the person's hand position, but the hand itself is obscured from view. For some tests the goal is simply speed, for others, accuracy. In one study, Sainburg only shows the cursor momentarily before it disappears, forcing the subject to move to the target without seeing his hand or the cursor. If you guessed that one hand performs more erratically than the other, you're correct. But if you thought the "strong" hand is the superior performer, think again.

In fact, each arm performs better depending on the goal. The dominant arm gets to the target more efficiently, but the nondominant arm is more accurate. Sainburg's interpretation of these results goes like this: Because the dominant arm-brain team better anticipates the forces invoked during the movement, it can make smoother, more energy-efficient movements. Nondominant arm movement isn't as smooth, but it lands on the target with greater accuracy. "So if you simply want to get to a location, use the nondominant arm," says Sainburg. "If you want to make a movement with a specific shape and speed, like throwing something at a target, use the dominant arm."

But how is it that the supposedly awkward, weaker, nondominant side can be better at anything? Asymmetry in hand performance is not about strength. The nondominant arm, unless you're Pete Sampras, is not weaker, despite the antiquated idea that hand preference is determined by subconsciously electing the stronger of the two arms or hands to be the preferred one. In fact, when carrying out certain motions, muscles of the nondominant arm sometimes exert more force than the same muscles of the dominant one because the latter one is better at moving in a fluid, energy-efficient manner.

Based on this model, one arm is specialized for controlling trajectory, or the shape and speed of a movement. The dominant system—i.e., the right arm for righties and the left arm for lefties—is the planner, wired to the more sophisticated motion-mapping capabilities within the brain. Eye on the nail, lifting of the arm, and piston-like motion with the forearm to deliver about 15 pounds of force equals nail into wall. Of course we never think this way, but that's the idea of modeling biomechanics.

The nondominant system, meanwhile, is charged with limb posture. That is, bracing a loaf of bread while the other hand slices with a knife, holding the nail while the other hand swings the hammer, or squeezing a jar while the other hand twists the lid. The nondominant hand may not paint you a Monet, but according to Sainburg's theory, it's astutely responsive to sudden feedback, more so than the dominant hand. Each slice with the serrated knife or each blow with the hammer moves the loaf or the nail in small but significant ways, and it's the responsibility of the nondominant hand to respond to these changes quickly, steadying the ship. When subjects in the virtual reality setup had to correct their movements after an unexpected force, the nondominant arm performed better, presumably because of its superiority in stabilizing against the unexpected, whereas the traditionally dominant hand was executing a predetermined plan of attack and couldn't as easily alter its scripted course of action.

In the 1980s a French psychologist put forth the idea that an emphasis on left/right or dominant versus nondominant is, if not an all-out waste of time, at least not the best thing researchers should spend their time investigating.[10] Sainburg's theory of dynamic dominance goes further, suggesting that neither hand is the weaker nor the lesser, but that they're specialized for different functions, and this specialization offers greater overall coordination of the two. It's not just that our hands do most operations in concert—typing, sewing, swinging a baseball bat, tying shoelaces, etc.—it's that our hands do complementary things. In Sainburg's view, and his research supports this hypothesis, each arm is charged with different responsibilities.

When discussing bimanual coordination, scientists sometimes refer to a waiter carrying a tray and what is called the "barman effect." Take a drink off a tray, and the waiter is likely to dump the rest of its contents in your lap. But a waiter can independently unload the tray item by item without any problems because the brain and limbs exquisitely share and coordinate information about weight change and timing. Sainburg's dynamic dominance model could also be applied to this example. The traditionally dominant hand is assigned the task of unloading the drinks, but the other hand has an equally important role of holding and balancing the tray as the weight and weight distribution change.

Sainburg recalls an experience one summer afternoon that helped him interpret findings from the lab. He was throwing a baseball with his oldest son to help him warm up before a game. A right-hander, Sainburg had forgotten his glove that day and was switching back and forth between catching the ball with his bare left and right hands. Gradually, he noticed that his left hand was getting sore, but his right hand was not. As he thought about it, he theorized that his dominant right-arm-left-brain system was better at anticipating the arriving ball, careful to let it carry his arm backward in a pre-planned cradling motion to reduce sudden impact. His left hand, by this point red and smarting, couldn't anticipate or plan nearly as well.

Where left-handedness fits into this scheme, Sainburg isn't exactly sure, and when I spoke with him about dynamic dominance, he was just beginning studies involving left-handed subjects. Although hesitant to speculate until the data are in, when pressed, Sainburg thinks that left-handers will express the opposite control patterns from those expressed by right-handers: "It shouldn't matter which side takes on the trajectory function, and which side takes on the stabilization functions, as long as the same separation of responsibilities occurs." It's the separation to optimize coordination that matters, not the direction of that separation. Sainburg, like Annett, thinks a genetic factor may be the instigator for right-hand bias, but in his view the force driving the population-wide trait is not about brain sidedness for something like speech but rather for coordination advantage.

If that's the case, then Hopkins's discovery of chimp bias for right-handedness would make sense.

During evolution, brain lateralization of functions in one or the other hemisphere gradually, through eons of accident and selection, bestowed upon us better brain efficiency. "I believe the drive to be handed is the drive to be coordinated," says Sainburg. "Long ago, one or more genes for right-handedness may have yielded a coordination advantage, and so it stuck."[11] That bias could just as easily have been to the left hand and right hemisphere, but it didn't happen that way. Because lefties and mixed-handers persist in the human population, Sainburg suspects that either "the selective pressure for more exquisite coordination may no longer be with us as our societies become more technologically advanced," or there's an ulterior evolutionary advantage to having non–right-handers in the population that no one has yet pinpointed.

In raising the possibility of coordination-catalyzed handedness, Sainburg has thrown yet another wrench into the already belching machinery of handedness theory. Recent studies with brain scans support the notion, however, tying handedness to motor control more than to language.[12] Unfortunately, left-handedness doesn't easily fit that model, which leaves Sainburg, his 12-year-old left-handed son, and me more than a little perplexed. But if the roots of handedness are in coordination, and if traces of that coordination can be seen in overhand-throwing chimps, Sainburg has at least one new friend in Bill Hopkins—or 91 new friends, if you count the Yerkes chimps.

———— • ◆ • ————

Back in Atlanta, overlooking the chimpanzees now munching on chunks of cantaloupe, I think about why Hopkins's findings strike a chord of common sense. For one thing, the idea that chimps might be a little more like us with their handedness tendencies than, for instance, rats suggests a more graduated view of evolution, to borrow a term from the late Stephen Jay Gould. That is, certain traits and behaviors developed incrementally, compared to the sudden arrival of speech and right-handedness, catapulting humans onto an island of uniqueness, biblical undertones and all. What primate research may ultimately teach us about handedness, and human evolution more broadly, is that whatever process was at work to make us such lateralized-minded creatures, that same process may very well have been at work, though to a less dramatic degree, in our evolutionary predecessors.

To emphasize further the utter unoriginality of brain asymmetry, consider for a moment recent discoveries about octopuses that apparently favor use of one eye over the other. As Eric Scigliano writes in a 2003 *Discover* article about these underestimated marine animals: "Such lateralization, corresponding to our right- and left-handedness, suggests specialization in the brain's hemispheres, which is believed to improve its efficiency and which was first considered an exclusively human, then an exclusively vertebrate, attribute."[13]

Contrast these findings of brain asymmetry and left- or right-side bias in other creatures with the Right Shift Theory, which has a genetic agent triggering a monumental shift in the brain allowing for speech function to emerge in the left hemisphere *and*, simultaneously, a bias toward right-handedness. Although the Right Shift Theory may yet prove to be correct, one could argue that nature "creating" a behavior like handedness with a sudden snap of its fingers doesn't sound as probable. As neurobiologist Calvin writes: "behavior invents and adaptation via gene changes makes the invention more efficient."[14] Could throwing have been one such behavior, and could gene changes leading to handedness have subsequently made it a more efficient and elaborate invention? As that adaptation led to more unevenness in the brain, did spoken communication come next?

McManus's theory of random cerebral variation also runs into trouble when facing off against Hopkins's team of chimps, although there may be room for the two to coexist. Hemispheric dominance for language isn't at issue because the thrust of McManus's theory is that a gene, through additional cerebral shuffling, acts directly on hand preference. But he also thinks that this hypothetical gene for more varied brain organization is a recent arrival on the human genome. If Socrates, Mega, and some of the other chimps at Yerkes are left-handed—or even just *somewhat* left-handed—McManus's theory, as he clearly stated when I dropped in on him in London, is wrong.

"I think Hopkins has been clever in exploiting natural behaviors to engage in and dig into the handedness question," says Lauren Harris at Michigan State University. "There are still skeptics who believe that you can make the case on the individual level but that it's hard to make the case at the species level. But Hopkins is moving us in the direction of accepting that there's a population-level bias for right-handedness in chimpanzees."

But where does that leave lefties? Shooting down the Right Shift Theory and providing evidence of population-wide bias for right-handedness in chimps unsettles other potential explanations for right- and left-handedness, but then what? Driving in his Honda to the field station, Hopkins turns down the volume of a Grateful Dead CD and, with the frustrating humility of a scientist who recognizes the boundaries of knowledge, gets to the point. As far as what makes people left-handed, he says, "I don't think anyone has an answer for you." But he does introduce some ideas I'd previously discounted.

Until now, I'd given up on the potential impact of such environmental factors as birth stress or biochemistry in the womb, in part because genetic theories seem so reasonable, and in part because environment-based hypotheses have a habit of flopping. But it goes without saying that I'm also turned off by these theories because of my own bias against any notion remotely suggestive of the idea that left-handedness might result from some developmental process gone awry.

Yet some of Hopkins's more recent data force the issue. For instance, he's found a strong correlation between birth order and handedness. First-born chimps, as well as chimps with many older siblings, are statistically more likely to be left-handed or, in that careful wordiness of the laterality business, more likely to show left-hand preference for certain tasks.* If that's true, it reintroduces questions of prenatal conditions in the womb affecting handedness.

For chimps and humans alike, first-time childbirth is far more traumatic for both mother and child. Maybe something that happens at birth *is* influencing handedness, despite the

---

*Hopkins's research indicates that more than 50 percent of chimps with five or more older siblings are left-handed.

earlier rejection of Geschwind's idea about *in utero* testosterone levels. Older mothers are also more likely to have pregnancy complications, and infants with many older siblings are more likely to have older moms. Similarly, Hopkins has identified a potential correlation between handedness and the mother's hormonal activity during pregnancy as measured by swelling of the reproductive region—an interesting find, although I'm glad it's him and not me taking measurements.

Hopkins rattles off quick summaries of these and other studies, not as a crescendo to any definitive declaration or blockbuster theory about the cause of handedness, but rather to emphasize correlations that at least deserve our attention. With other predominant theories overturned or facing new challenges, surely there's room for discussion about new possibilities.

"Lefties are always interesting, I guess," he tells me on the drive back to campus. "Some people argue that you do or don't have the right-handed gene. . . . But the human data on left-handedness just is not very sophisticated. Personally, I don't believe there's a clear right- or left-handedness," he says, almost as an afterthought. "I think it's a continuum."

· CHAPTER 8 ·

Brainwriting

There's always a bias to explain things positively.
Even if there's dozens of negative results, people,
including scientists, seek out the positive ones,
even if the negative ones might be correct.[1]

—*Marian Annett*

All these links between handedness and communication keep surfacing: Broca's discovery of the brain's speech center; the Right Shift Theory's possible connection to language; and chimps sending messages through the air in the form of flying sticks and excrement. But another form of communication is perhaps most critical to the left-hander's experience: the act of writing.

Few aspects of the lefty world are as essential to the Southpaw identity as handwriting and its corollaries of hand posture; legibility; and, for some people, smudging. How we hold a pen and paper is usually how lefties spot one another. You don't see someone with a wine glass in the left hand and say: "Hey, you're lefty—me too." Writing is up there with throwing a curveball as far as primary qualifications for Southpaw status go, at least in Western societies. Aside from the large population of lefties who in the past were forced to write with the right hand, few people nowadays who write with the right hand would be so bold as to claim that they're Southpaws.

Two prominent laterality researchers once postulated that lefties writing with the hooked-hand style had speech lateralized in the left hemisphere of the brain, whereas those writing with the more common posture of pen below the line of text had their speech center in the right hemisphere. Broca would have enjoyed the asymmetry discussion, but unfortunately writing posture proved to be an ineffective indicator of brain sidedness.[2]

Nevertheless, because writing is a core component of the left-hander essence, I wanted to know what handwriting specialists say about lefties and the influence of handedness on writing and, in turn, personality. Could there be differences in the personalities of people who use the tensed-up, hooked-hand posture versus the slanted-notepad approach versus the rare pen and paper position that actually looks "normal"—in the righty sense of the word? And can so-called graphologists really make inferences about character based on a person's penmanship?

———•◆•———

To begin the weekend conference, we turn to a sample passage on page 4 of our manual, *Handwriting Analysis 101.* The paragraph of text is written in a chaotic, crowded, barely legible scrawl. Bart Baggett, president of Handwriting University, asks: "Would you let this person date your daughter?"

A murmur of "no"s and even a couple "no way"s oscillate through the room.

Baggett: "Who here is a complete beginner?"

I raise my hand.

"David. Step up to the microphone."

I'm facing an audience of 50 or so people in a basement seminar room in the Crystal City Hyatt in Crystal City, Virginia. Many of the attendees are sporting navy-blue Handwriting University sweatshirts.

Baggett: "This is the best—this is my favorite handwriting sample. Do you have kids, David?"

With my back to him, speaking into the microphone and pointing my face toward the video camera as instructed, I say no.

Baggett: "You don't have kids. If you did, would you let that person date your daughter?" By "that person" he means the unlucky soul who wrote the passage on page 4 of the handbook, who, I later learn, is a convicted felon still serving his sentence at Arizona State Prison.

"No."

Baggett: "Why not?"

"Because I wrote it," I quip.

The room explodes in laughter, and I instantly get a surge of confidence because now I'm the New Witty Guy. The feeling won't last.

Baggett, laughing with the group: "He can stay!"

———◆———

When I first learned about Handwriting University, I was curious about two selling points. One was a detailed analysis of the writing on the now-famous envelope used to deliver anthrax to Senators Daschle and Leahy in 2001, an episode that resulted in a wave of tabloid exposure for Baggett. The other was the promise that, with Handwriting University training, I would be able to understand the complex personality of Michael Jackson through examination of his penmanship.

After signing up for the seminar, I began receiving weekly e-newsletter messages, often with a new featured article: "Is Your Boss a Big Fat Liar?" "Do You Write Like a Self-Made Millionaire?" "The Terrors and Tribulations of Being Involved with Someone with a Delicate 'd.'" "Are You in Control or a Control Freak?" "Today, Take 8 Minutes and Discover a Jerk's Handwriting by the Way He Makes a T-Bar."

When Baggett was 14, he caught on to graphology after his father began studying it at home in Dallas, Texas. Now the younger Baggett lives in Hollywood and hopes to earn a spot as a television game show host. Just before I arrived in Crystal City, he'd been featured on *Court TV* to discuss the handwriting of then-accused murderer Scott Peterson. If the insight into human behavior resulting from graphology knowledge is even a fraction as powerful as Baggett and his followers claim, this weekend may turn out to be more valuable for me than four years of college.

The first lesson of the introductory lecture includes a list of attributes that cannot be inferred from handwriting, which include age, gender, and—crap!—handedness. Baggett puts it like this: "Left-handed people basically compensate, but their perception is, 'I slant backwards because I'm left-handed.' No, that's not correct. There's plenty of left-handed people that tilt their hand this way [he hooks his hand like a claw] and they write. Have you seen this? And they have an E+ slant [i.e., tilted far to the right] and you're like 'oh my god how do they do that?' Or they tilt the paper sideways. They compensate if they're well adjusted."

He's not quite done, though: "Now, if they're emotionally withdrawn because they've had trauma, because they've had sexual molestation, because they've had other issues that aren't resolved yet, that's why their handwriting tilts to the back. That's why they've got that backward slant."

In spite of this early leveling of handedness as a nonissue for handwriting analysis, I still need convincing. For one thing, I don't understand Baggett's explanation about compensating. Compensating for what? Plus, I can't yet jettison the idea that how one holds a pen and the mechanics of writing do influence penmanship, or at least influence penmanship *a little*. And if penmanship is a window into personality—"handwriting is brainwriting," as they say in the trade—left-handedness's impact on writing could alter or possibly corrupt a graphologist's analysis for a rather large chunk of the literate human population. And so I hold out on drawing any conclusions until I've learned more.

The seminars proceed with explanations of some of the more pronounced and significant penmanship traits, including stroke slant and major indictors embedded in certain letter formations. The more right-leaning the slant, for example, the more open, emotional, passionate, and action-driven the person. I also learn about individual letter traits: double loop on the "o" of someone concealing the truth; A-frame legs to the letter "t" indicating stubbornness; upward slope to the "m" showing self-consciousness; downturned "y" and/or "g" revealing a fear of success.

What I like most about the conference are the breaks, in part because they're spiced up with tunes like the Chumbawamba hit single "Tub Thumping"—*I get knocked down, but I get up again!*—and in part because it gives me a chance to chat it up with conference attendees. As soon as I walked in the first morning, I met Stan Levin and Ed Levien, two Bethesda guys who're also lefties, which I learn only because I overhear one of them counting how many lefties are here this weekend (six people out of 50, as far as I can tell). No right-handers would ever do this—why would they?—and I decide that I like these two guys immediately.

Among the participants are some nice old women, some younger blonde women, and a shorter woman from Calgary who gives me some fruit. There's the golfer guy from Chicago and the physical education teacher from New York State, and the aloof dude from L.A. There's also an Asian-looking man with a Russian-sounding name and his good friend, an older black woman with frosty hair who, in their friendship, remind me why it's still OK to love this country.

One reason I don't fall asleep during the sessions is that sex and relationships are by far the dominant themes. Baggett is full of one-liners about the long, wide letter "y" dangling down to indicate sexual energy, and he is quick to reference female genitalia after someone asks about the "mound" shape to look for on a particular letter stroke. Graphology, after all, is especially useful when looking for potential lovers or analyzing one's ex, which may be why the sessions consistently touch on traits such as compatibility, stubbornness, sexual and physical energy, and sexual imagination.

During the evening cocktail hour I share a few beers with an unassuming financial adviser from Chicago and the guy who sits in the auditorium front row, nodding nonstop throughout the lectures. The Nodder is a lefty who works for the Navy in some intelligence office capacity. He recently had what sounds like a horrible bout with strep that laid him out for two months with little to do but read, and before long he was hooked on handwriting analysis. Since then, the Nodder has analyzed the handwriting of 143 people. "I've only seen one who was clearly a nymphomaniac. I didn't tell her that, of course. I just said she was probably a real fun date." Before long, I'm roped in to being examinee number 144.

He hands me a homemade printout for recording writing samples, on which I sign my name and copy the following sentence: "I know said the purple people eater; you and your silly monkey don't go home to the zoo." At the bottom is his contact information and the tagline: "Mr. Write."

The analysis is a deluge of questions about my goals, my relationship with my parents, my sense of self-esteem, whether I work well in a team, whether I hold strong to my opinions, whether I'm considered a good listener. They are leading—"Would you say that your parents are critical of you? No, not really? OK. Let's move on."—though generally innocuous. For the most part I enjoy hearing his satisfaction when I answer yes—"Do you consider yourself independent-minded?"—or watching him steam ahead unfazed when I answer no. In the end, about half of his inferences are, in the loosest sense of the word, correct.

Although the Nodder and others will compliment me on the intelligence, directness, "fluidity of thought," and even impressive sex drive they see manifest in my handwriting, this is where I finally lose patience. Not because they're talking about life under the sheets, but because their certainty is reminiscent of zealots the world over, and it's both annoying and creepy. To be honest, I tune out a little toward the end of his "analysis," instead watching his face for a hint of doubt, maybe a smirk. But his bright eyes, large nose, and wide jaw reveal nothing but a jovial disposition and absolute conviction.

The following day we learn about the undesirable trait of "backwards," meaning left-leaning penmanship, from seasoned analyst Don Lehew of Dallas. Left-leaning handwriting indicates, among other things, the writer is egocentric, aloof, stuck up, standoffish, withdrawn, stubborn, narcissistic, distrustful, and likely to dwell in the past. And I almost forgot: left-leaners are also more likely to be women.

During the lecture, I recall something I'd read about poet Walt Whitman's observations during the Civil War. Noting how injured, right-handed soldiers were learning to write with the left hand, Whitman, then working as a nursing orderly, wrote: "A great many of the specimens are written in a beautiful manner. All are good. The writing in nearly all cases slants backwards instead of forward."[3] Apparently Whitman had no knowledge of just how bad backwards slant can be.

The next day, seeking some like-handed company, I manage to corner Levin and Levien for lunch, and we convince Baggett to sit with us and talk about left-handedness. He begins by saying he'd bet more left-handed people have a backward slant than right-handed people. It's a manifestation, he explains, of the psychological impact from living within a society where left-handers are ostracized, therefore making lefties emotionally introverted. "It has nothing to do with holding the pen funny."

For the record, I have a strong forward slant to my writing, but this part about lefties more often being back-slanters confuses me. It contradicts, for one thing, what *Handwriting Analysis 101* says about "only a small percentage of left-handed people slant[ing] to the left." Yet if handedness is irrelevant in the relay of personality from brain to page, then these back-slanting lefties Baggett is talking about would also more often be terrible women. Unfortunately, this point doesn't exactly mesh with more credible studies about gender and handedness, all of which indicate that the percentage of men who're Southpaws is slightly higher than the percentage of lefty women.[4] Then again, this is a weekend of *Twilight Zone* logic, where contradictions are prohibited from interfering with smooth talk.

Baggett, Levin, Levien, and I munch on barbecue chicken sandwiches and Caesar salads. But I can't hold back the questions for long, and ask again—just in a different way— why handedness doesn't relate to the "science" of handwriting analysis.

"So let me ask you a question," says Baggett. "If you lost both your hands in an accident and had to write with your feet, and you wrote enough that you actually learned how to do it, what slant would show up?"

"I don't know."

I tell him that if I had to write with my feet, I honestly don't know what slant I would have. But I would probably strive for a right slant because I find it more aesthetically pleasing.

Baggett, impatiently: "What's your natural slant?"

Levin, on my behalf: "He's a DE." DE is one of the slant ratings used by graphologists.

Baggett: "If you're a DE, your feet would be DE. Is it brainwriting or handwriting?"

"Uh, it's foot-writing."

Baggett, a little irritated: "Well, it's brainwriting. And the hand is the conduit that you learn how to do it with. There are people that have never had hands that write. It comes out like handwriting. And it's a reflection of their brains."

"So mine would definitely be right-leaning?"

Baggett, stabbing at his iced-tea with a straw: "If you had enough time to do it, yeah, absolutely. I mean, it could be sloppy at first, but yes, absolutely."

I have another question. The thing is, I begin, as a left-hander, I often cross my "t"s backwards (i.e., from right to left). I show him an example of this on my notepad. But we learned in class that more ink on the left side of the trunk indicates procrastination or laziness, and more ink on the right side indicates short temper.

"Anger," interrupts Levin.

I press ahead. "So if I'm coming at it from the right side, could I have a tendency to deliver more ink on this [right] side of the "t" than on this [left] side? Could that be misinterpreted as a temper even though I'm not—"

Handwriting analysts put a lot of stock in tiny strokes, not to mention collect a lot of money from people who want to learn what each stroke means. If I'm going to make inferences about someone else's personality, be it a trait like laziness, short temper, or anything, I want to be spot-on correct. What's more, I feel compelled to ask this stuff on behalf of Southpaws. Because while Baggett and his flock claim that "proof of ability is results" and that handwriting analysis is between 98 and 100 percent accurate, I need to be doubly sure that scores of left-handers crossing their "t's" like me aren't being misread.

Baggett: "Great, great question. And, I gotta tell you that I don't know. I don't know if my answer is right because I haven't researched enough to know that. . . . But again, listen: if it [the stroke direction] is going back into yourself and it's a temper, then you're probably not going to show it to other people. So then it stacks another trait into the situation going 'well, there's a temper, but it's all going into yourself,' so it's self-critical temper. So you may have a short fuse about yourself but you may not show it to somebody else."

I tell him I think he's speaking too fast for me.

"Me too," says Baggett coldly, turning to face Levien.

I have one final chance to question Baggett before he leaves our company. As far as personality goes, do you find there are things about left-handers that are different?

"I have no evidence of that," he says, clearly exasperated. "You know why? It never crosses my mind. I don't care. It's not in the writing. I never ask. Therefore I would be the wrong person to ask because I've done no research on it. It's not significant to me."

The conversation goes blank.

Baggett: "If it makes you feel better, though, I'll tell you that [lefties] are smarter than the average person." And with that, he excuses himself from our table.

———— •◆• ————

Nearly three months later, I get a notice from the Multnomah County elections office here in Portland. Oregon is a vote-by-mail state, and apparently the signature on my voter registration card was sufficiently different from the one on the back of the envelope containing my ballot as to require a supplementary example before the ballot could be counted on election day. County officials spared me an evaluation of personality changes evident from the two different signatures, but I shudder to think what the graphologists among them might be thinking.

CHAPTER 9

Renegade

Reason is our soul's left hand, Faith her right.[1]

—*John Donne, "To the Countess of Bedford"*

Tail between my legs, I return home from my foray into the world of graphology, only to pack my bags again. I'm off to Ohio this time, to meet a researcher who will completely upend my thinking about handedness. After taking for granted that 10–12 percent of the population is left-handed, it's perhaps unfair of me at this point to suggest that this figure is off—way off. If you feel misled, I sympathize. "We've been thinking about handedness wrong for the last 150 years," says University of Toledo psychology professor Stephen Christman.

The differences we should be investigating, argues Christman, are not those found between right- and left-handers but between strong- and mixed-handed people. Based on this premise, those who are strongly right- or strongly left-handed make up one subgroup and total half the human population, whereas mixed-handed people make up the other half. Put another way, the essential handedness distinction is not direction, but degree.

"Few others have thought about this left-brain/right-brain stuff from this perspective. I'm a good enough scientist to know that I could be wrong. But if I keep rolling to 2010 with more evidence supporting this idea, then I think I'll start to get cockier."[2] If his novel theory of handedness turns out to be correct, Christman, as much as if not more than Hopkins and his chimps, could revolutionize not only *what* is understood about handedness but also *how* handedness is understood.

I'm a good example of a strong left-hander in that I use my left hand for 10 out of 10 tasks on the Edinburgh Handedness Inventory. Someone who's the exact opposite, preferring the right hand for virtually all tasks, is a strong right-hander. Although he writes with his left hand, Christman says he's mixed-handed, sometimes pitting his left hand against his right in solo games of darts at home in his basement. All those people who have mixed preference—showing 5–5, 7–3, or even 9–1 breakdowns on the EHI—Christman would consider mixed-handed.

Christman isn't the first to call into question the indestructibility of the right/left dichotomy. About 20 years ago, researchers began to note that many people, categorized as lefties because the left was their preferred hand for writing, in fact preferred throwing with the right hand. Such findings suggest people aren't necessarily one or the other.[3] In a way, this anti-dichotomous thinking echoes what Sainburg argues, namely that the hands interact in a complementary manner, not in a relationship based on rigid notions of dominant versus nondominant.

Because a few select motor skills—primarily writing, throwing, and eating—are usually the default indicators of handedness within most societies, and because we've been trained to identify ourselves with either the lefty or righty camp, this notion of being mixed- versus strong-handed is a little difficult to accept. It would mean millions of people who've always assumed they're right-handed because they use the right hand for chopping, writing, and brushing, may in fact be mixed-handed. The same would go for a smaller group of people previously known as lefties. (Keep in mind that mixed-handed is not synonymous with ambidextrous.)

Nor is Christman the first to suggest that handedness rests on a sliding scale, a cornerstone of Annett's Right Shift Theory. In her original model, people either have the gene conferring right-handedness, or they become mixed-handed. (Some researchers contend that Annett leaves out of the model the estimated 2–3 percent of the population who're strongly left-handed.) The hypothetical handedness gene in Christman's theory acts similarly, turning almost half the population into strong right-handers, only 2–3 percent into strong left-handers, and the other half into mixed-handers.

Christman breaks trail when he ties strong- versus mixed-handedness to an anatomical feature of the brain, asserting that any differences between right- and left-handers are trumped by more significant differences evident between strong- and mixed-handers. He points to decades of minimal-gains psychology research about the differences between lefties and righties as de facto support for this degree-not-direction concept. That research has, for the most part, failed to turn up major differences between righties and lefties.

But a theory constructed on the fallacies of other theories isn't much of a theory. Christman's own hypothesis began to take shape in the 1980s, when he read a paper about a possible correlation between corpus callosum size and handedness *strength*. Again, the corpus callosum is the cable-like structure linking the brain's left and right hemispheres. The paper suggested that the stronger the person's handedness bias for one side or the other, the smaller the corpus callosum.

The second clue came in a report on failed efforts to breed mice with left- or right-paw preference. After breeding 15 or more generations, scientists found that each new mouse still had a 50–50 chance of being left- or right-pawed. This kind of result was critical for ideas about population-wide right bias being a uniquely human phenomenon. The researchers could, however, breed for mice with either strong- or mixed-paw preference, suggesting that degree of handedness might be an inherited trait.

Next Christman wondered what kind of effect variable corpus callosum size might have on human motor function. Could there be differences from person to person in how the two sides of the brain communicate? If the bundle of nerve fibers ferrying communiqués between the hemispheres is larger in some people than in others, might those people also demonstrate superior performance with the exchange of information? Conversely, if the corpus callosum were smaller, wouldn't that mean better shielding between the hemispheres when trying to conduct two tasks simultaneously?

To test his theory, he first compared left- and right-handed musicians. The key was the instruments people chose to play, which Christman broke into three categories: he lumped keyboard and percussion instruments together because the two hands follow independent lines of music that are meant to "speak" simultaneously; string and woodwind instruments emphasize precise integration of hand coordination, such as the intricate interplay between a violinist's fingers on one hand and the movement of the bow in the other; and then horn instruments, which are essentially played one-handed, or at least one hand performs most of the sophisticated action.

In previous studies, left-handers proved to be more mixed-brain under certain circumstances, whereas right-handers showed more pronounced one-sidedness of brain function. That distinction will get more play in a later discussion, but for now the key is that Christman used it to predict that among a large enough population of musicians, he would find lefties more likely playing string and woodwind instruments, which require more cross-brain interaction. Right-handers, meanwhile, would more likely be inclined to play keyboard and percussion instruments, capitalizing on the brain's ability to block out distracting noise.

When the data came back from a sample of 170 musicians, "the numbers were a total wash." The problem was that Christman was still under the influence of the old-school notion of left versus right. Not only that, but he was overlooking the fact that the number of true lefties in the population is quite small; most people who identify themselves as left-handers are actually mixed-handers in disguise, yet Christman had not made any attempt to differentiate these people among his sample of musicians.

The breakthrough came a few weeks later when listening to a friend warm up on the drums. "With his left arm and foot he played a nice, 4–4 rhythm. Then with his right arm and foot, he was doing a 3–4 waltz beat—at the same time! I couldn't do that. When I sit at the drums, I have no independence over my limbs." The drummer, he also knew, was strongly right-handed. Christman suddenly suspected that his friend's strong-handedness "effectively shielded" left- and right-hemisphere activity from interfering with each other, thus facilitating the schizoid drum playing. In contrast, the two sides of Christman's own brain, as a mixed-hander, are "too yoked together to do that."

A smaller corpus callosum for strong-handers and a larger one for mixed-handers matches up, at least in theory, with this observed behavior. When Christman went back and retooled the numbers from the musicians study, this time looking for strong-handedness in either direction of the continuum, the data showed a significant correlation between degree of handedness and chosen musical instruments. "That was the beginning of my realization that it's not left versus right but mixed versus strong."

The gargantuan implications of his statement leave me dumbstruck. If he's right, nearly all scientists—to say nothing of societies—have been incorrectly carving up the handedness pie into groups of lefties and righties instead of "strongs" and "mixeds." What's wilder still is that if Southpaws aren't a distinct group, my quest could be fundamentally unresolvable; either that or I've just been handed the makings for a sequel.

After publishing his findings, Christman knew he would be challenged, and rightly so; further studies were needed. But as far as degree versus direction, he was sold. Around that same time, researchers in Düsseldorf demonstrated varying asymmetry in the brains of musicians and nonmusicians. As reported in *New Scientist* magazine, "non-musicians had the largest asymmetry or discrepancy between their hands; string musicians a smaller asymmetry; and keyboard players the least of all."[4] Could a large corpus callosum allow the two sides of the brain to communicate more, and vice versa for a smaller corpus callosum?

Interest in strong- versus mixed-handedness is gaining ground as attention shifts from an emphasis on left versus right hands, to asymmetrical versus symmetrical brains. In many subsequent studies, Christman and other scientists have successfully predicted that for tasks requiring the two hands to cooperate, mixed-handers do better, whereas for tasks requiring the hands to perform separately, strong-handers do better. Strong left-handers are hard to come by and therefore hard to study, but from what little data are available, true Southpaws seem to perform better on the same independent-hand tasks that strong right-handers do, like tapping out two different drum beats simultaneously.

In raising these questions, Christman foresaw accusations of quackery on the horizon. For one thing, any supposition about brain function based on anatomy can get people thinking about things like eugenics and *Brave New World*. But the other problem for Christman is that his theory, although centered on *communication* between the hemispheres and not *characterization* of the hemispheres, nevertheless reminds researchers of public perceptions about the two sides of the brain that have drifted disappointingly far from sound science.

Beginning in the 1960s, neurosurgeons performed a rare and radical procedure, cutting the corpus callosum as a last-resort treatment for severe epilepsy. Even though the operation was, as aggressive procedures go, moderately successful, the real windfall was not in the treatment of epilepsy but in neuroscience. Split-brain patients, as they came to be known, offered a window into the lateralized workings of the brain, an inside view that had previously been beyond the reach of science. Studies with the split-brain patients led to a Nobel Prize for Caltech's Roger Sperry in 1981, and decades of research on only a handful of individuals has revealed an astonishing amount of information about the operations of the mind and how the two sides function, both separately and in tandem.

It's because of the split-brain patients that we know, in simplified terms, that emotion sits to the right, reason to the left; visual and spatial perception are strongly represented in the right; and the list goes on, although any such run-down is crude, if not misleading, for it will inevitably belie the brain's complexity. "What happens inside your head is more like an orchestra than a soloist, with dozens of players contributing to the overall mix," writes Steven Johnson in *Mind Wide Open*. Rarely are all those players situated exclusively on one side of the brain.[5] As another expert puts it: "There is almost nothing that is regulated solely by the left or right hemisphere."[6]

Unfortunately, information featuring split-brain studies was poorly conveyed to the public, or the public was poorly equipped to receive it, or both. As a result, many people couldn't fully comprehend the origins and context of these profound findings, and extrapolation about hemispheric differences got way out of hand. Caltech's Joseph E. Bogen, one of the original pioneers of the split-brain operations, explains: "The media pushed the popularity of the 'right brain/left brain' story to fad proportions, reaching an almost frenzied peak by 1980. This led not only to simplistic degradation, probably inevitable with popularization, but also to exploitation."[7] The public wasn't fully aware of just how impaired the split-brain patients were, in terms of coordination as well as some cognitive functions. Most people also failed to grasp how critical the corpus callosum is for cohesive brain operations, and perhaps most overlooked of all, how integrated and in many ways interdependent the two sides of the brain really are.

Using this research, pseudoscientists began adding 2 and 2 together to get 5, then charging people $185 an hour for insight about the hemispheres. If the right side of the brain plays quarterback for emotion and spatially related tasks, then left-handed people, whose arms are controlled by the motor cortex on the right side of the brain, must surely be better artists or, as we've so often heard, more creative. Conversely, left-brain people should go into professions like accounting. All this "neuro-mythology" was carried so far at one point that it led to practices like seating mathematics-inclined students on the right side of classrooms to open up their more "artistic brains," or instructing people to doodle with the nondominant hand to further access the brain's supposedly untapped reservoir of creativity. This legacy of misinformation continues to this day, irking the bejeezus out of the scientists who know better.

————•◆•————

When Christman was a graduate student at the University of California at Berkeley in the 1980s, he was fed, like most people, the conventional model for handedness: 10–12 percent of the population is left-handed. This was around the time when theories about left-handedness resulting from minor brain damage or abnormal biochemical conditions in the womb were in vogue. Skeptical of these emerging ideas and on the lookout for faulty conclusions about differences in intellect or left-handers' possible cognitive deficits, Christman's mentor, Curt Hardyck, assessed the handedness and IQ of a large sample of Bay Area high school students. He found *no* difference in IQ achievement levels between lefties and righties, although he did find lefties to be more variable in their scores.

By Christman's account, many researchers at that time were exasperated if not nauseated by the prospect of more handedness studies, believing that the topic was of overestimated merit. As a consequence, Christman was gently steered away from the subject for his dissertation research. But years later, when curiosity and serendipity combined to spark his interest once again in handedness, Christman found little had changed since his days back at Berkeley. The same professional allergy repelling psychologists from anything hinting at left-brain/right-brain distinctions was pervasive. "The right-brain mythology led to a generation of psychologists who thought left/right brain stuff was for crackpots."

Nowadays, conferences are filled with thousands of researchers reporting on high-tech imaging studies about particular operation centers of the brain that light up when subjects perform certain cognitive tasks. But it's simply written off as a given within this community, complains Christman, that the active corners of the brain under investigation are in one hemisphere or the other. The asymmetry is all but irrelevant. That the two hemispheres house vastly different operations is clear. Yet how they do or don't communicate and coordinate, and whether there might be quantifiable differences in that coordination between individuals or certain groups, are questions largely ignored, at least in Christman's reckoning, for fear of resurrecting ideas already tainted by left-brain/right-brain neuro-mythology.

The reality is probably not quite so extreme. Interest in localized areas within the hemispheres likely stems from stunning advances in our ability to hone in on those areas with ever more powerful technology, and less so out of apprehension about revisiting those persistent left/right fallacies. Still, the question of how those various modules interact, especially when passing information across the corpus callosum, may still be getting short shrift, particularly as the bounty of new knowledge about each control center makes it harder to uncover overarching principles of how the brain operates.

Along comes Christman and his idea of left/right difference—although his theory is about connectivity and not left- or right-brain "people"—and the response of contemporaries is annoyance or antipathy. One journal editor recently rejected a paper Christman submitted, which by itself is perfectly normal in the world of scientific publications. But when Christman wrote back to argue his case, or at least learn the rationale for rejection, the editor admitted that he'd jumped the gun because of an automatic bias against any research harkening back to those dark years of *Drawing on the Right Side of the Brain.*

Yet as Christman slowly chips away at this degree-not-direction theory, it may become increasingly difficult for peers to shun him. Other research connecting variation in brain structure to variation in cognition is further eroding this taboo. For instance, the corpus callosum is larger, on average, in women than in men, and neuroscientists are only beginning to untangle the implications of this difference.[8] Conversely, some brain studies suggest that men more easily move information around within each hemisphere.[9] Communication between the hemispheres, and differences in the structure that does that communicating, might play a more crucial role in brain function than people realize.

If corpus callosum size turns out to be the determinant of mixed- versus strong-handedness, it may do a lot more than implode any sense of lefty or righty identity; it may also influence cognition. Christman has set out to explore potential variation in brain activity that may relate to variation in corpus callosum size. Humans, after all, aren't manufactured on an assembly line. If each custom-built cable linking the two halves of the brain differs from person to person, it's reasonable to suppose that varied cables make for varied brain function. But might there be commonalities among certain groups, as identified by their handedness?

For example, researchers in Albany asked subjects to balance a dowel on a finger of the left hand while simultaneously repeating verbal phrases. Whereas the dowel balancing on the left is controlled by the right hemisphere, the verbal task is under the direction of the left hemisphere. ("It all comes back to Broca in the end.") Left-handers, a.k.a., mostly mixed-handers in disguise, showed more difficulty with the task because, so the theory goes, they had more interference between the two sides of their brains while trying to carry out the tasks simultaneously.

Another researcher applied the interhemispheric communication idea to older data suggesting that left-handed people are more likely to get into automobile accidents. Reworking the accident numbers to focus on degree not direction was easy because the same tool, the Edinburgh Handedness Inventory, is the instrument measure in each case.[10] The result fit impressively into Christman's model, with mixed-handers showing increased likelihood for accident trouble. Put another way, less cross-traffic in the brain may be an asset for people talking on a cell phone while driving, in the same way that it enables a drummer to play two different rhythms at once.

Christman and colleagues have also looked for this effect with regard to memory. In simplest terms, encoding of memories occurs in the left hemisphere, whereas retrieval of memories happens in the right. The prediction is that people with greater communication between the hemispheres, identified by mixed-handedness, should show greater memory recall compared to strong-handers. When subjects were asked the age of their earliest memories, which were later corroborated by interviews with parents, mixed-handers showed earlier recall. The average age of the earliest autobiographical memory of strong-handers in the study was 4.6 years old. For mixed-handers it was at 3.9 years. When asked to keep a diary of daily activities for a whole week and then two weeks later, without notes, recall the week's entries, mixed-handers again performed significantly better.

If degree of handedness is an indicator of interhemispheric communication, what else might be inferred in terms of differences between strong- and mixed-handers? I should emphasize that the idea of a larger corpus callosum for mixed-handed people remains a young one, but for Chris Niebauer at Slippery Rock University in Pennsylvania, it's a built-in assumption behind some thought-provoking research. Niebauer has taken the handoff from Christman and is delving into the idea that corpus callosum size—again revealed by degree of handedness—impacts some major areas of thinking.

At the risk of falling into the oversimplification trap my-self, think of the left hemisphere as the part of the brain that helps us shape a view of the world unaffected by minor varia-tion, allowing us to move through our daily lives with a rela-tive degree of normalcy and without constant anxiety over whether gravity, telephones, lungs, and the U.S Postal Ser-vice will function as anticipated. The right hemisphere, gen-erally speaking, is charged with keeping watch over variation or perturbation. When it reaches a sort of cognitive tipping point, the right hemisphere is responsible for updating the whole brain's big-picture beliefs.[11]

For instance, people may have held the belief, in their left hemispheres, that it was categorically impossible for the Boston Red Sox to win a World Series. Eighty-six years' worth of evidence would have supported that belief, with no major perturbation or contrary data threatening the status quo. But after the Sox's 2004 season, the brain's right hemisphere should have stepped in to override the left hemisphere's out-dated belief. Without the updating function of the right hemisphere, it's possible the left hemisphere would find some bizarre way to justify its old paradigm in spite of new data, such as insisting that the Red Sox victory was a hoax staged, by television studio technicians. As weird as this may sound, some stroke patients suffering from a neurological condition known as anosognosia do exactly that, concocting elaborate stories to explain away information that cannot be incorpo-rated into their established worldview because the stroke has rendered the brain incapable of a paradigm overhaul.

If some people have better communication between the hemispheres as a result of structural differences in the corpus callosum, then is it possible to observe differences in people's ability to update their belief systems? And could handedness be a behavioral marker for this ability? Niebauer thinks so. Armed with admittedly imperfect surveys about handedness and attitudes toward such subjects as the supernatural and creation, he's come up with findings suggesting that mixed-handers are, for instance, more likely to believe in evolution. "One thing I was always interested in is why an intelligent adult would believe in creationism," says Niebauer. Most children, he explains, grow up with some sort of creation story; religious indoctrination aside, that's just how kids think. But as they get older, learning about evolution usually leads to an updating of beliefs about how the world and all its creatures came to be. Niebauer's numbers indicate that mixed-handed people tend to carry out this belief-updating more frequently than strong-handers.

It's not hard to see that the advantages and disadvantages of more or less cross-brain communication are different depending on the task at hand(s), as shown in the example of musical instruments. Nor is the human brain simple enough for blanket statements—mixed-handers are bad drivers and atheists, strong-handers are poor cellists and have weak memories—to have much currency. The brain is unfathomably complicated, not to mention varied from individual to individual, which means venturing into the question of different brain type characterizations is rooted in an effort to uncover trends, not to create pigeonholes. Even so, one researcher told me that he thinks Niebauer may have wandered into the old left-brain/right-brain pitfall.

It's possible, however, that the theory of varied interhemispheric communication based on corpus callosum size puts disproportionate trust into the late-'80s paper documenting correlation between size of this structure and degree of handedness. The problem is, until recently it was impossible to measure corpus callosum size in living subjects, and the technologies such as MRI that make it possible remain costly. That means handedness, at least for now, is often used as the proxy to separate people into different groups for these studies of interhemispheric communication, with the assumption that degree of handedness matches up with corpus callosum size. Still, asks Christman, what other component of the brain could possibly account for this variation in communication between its two sides? "I have a hard time thinking there's some kind of node in the hemispheres that teleports information between the two sides, but if someone shows it to me, then fine."

Christman also needs an explanation for the existence of strong left-handers in the population in light of the fact that his theory divides humanity into 50 percent mixed- and 50 percent strong-handed people. If only 2–3 percent of the population is made up of strong lefties like me, compared to approximately 47 percent strong right-handers, why the disproportion? Christman cites a number of studies showing that strong left-handers resemble strong right-handers more than they resemble mixed-handers, but the numbers are still confusing. He also acknowledges that the 2–3 percent of the population who are strongly left-handed probably *do* differ from strongly right-handed people in currently unknown ways, a tantalizing asterisk that will get more attention in a later section.

As a psychologist interested in asymmetries of the brain and their influence on behavior and cognition, Christman doesn't feel driven to come up with a theory that explains

left-handedness, but he has his suspicions: "I'm pretty convinced handedness is not caused by a single factor." But before
anyone can find a cause, it might help if someone first determines what is meant by handedness in terms of degree and
direction. For now, Christman is content to spend his time
working on this theory of mixed- versus strong-handedness
in relation to the broader idea of cross-brain communication
as a function of corpus callosum size. After asserting his hypothesis once again, he ends the interview by saying: "Maybe
in 10 years the University of Toledo will be your handedness
Mecca." And if people are skeptical of his idea, that's fine with
him: "If they're skeptical, it means they're paying attention."

Although Christman's work represents an unexpected
hairpin turn in this already winding journey, I find it inspiring
nevertheless. It's unconventional and cutting-edge and yes, it
may even be wrong. But there's a hunger for fresh answers in
Christman that I notice in myself. I leave Toledo with a
twisted satisfaction about how perplexing this search has become, wondering just how far down the rabbit hole goes.

· CHAPTER 10 ·

The Spinster

Oh, vain is all our striving, our yearning is folly,
until we have determined which is right and left . . . [1]

———————

—*Karl Marx*

When I'd asked Chris McManus where the left-handers'
Mecca might be, his first answer was Paris because
of Broca. His second choice was Nobutaka Hirokawa's lab
in Tokyo. At Tokyo University School of Medicine, I find
the office suite of Hirokawa, a man with one of those not-
so-shabby titles on his business card: dean of the Graduate
School of Medicine, professor and chair of the department of
cell biology and anatomy. Hanging on the wall are a dozen or
so framed covers from such prestigious journals as *Cell*, *Science*, and *Neuron*, all from issues featuring Hirokawa's work.
One of his recent discoveries may be the foundation for all
asymmetry in the body, including handedness.[2]

The famous scientist is wearing a grape-colored button-
down shirt. He gives me a quick hello, guides me to one of
two wide leather chairs, sits down in the other one, and immediately begins describing his research with the aid of a

presentation on his laptop computer. The human brain is unequivocally and profoundly uneven; Broca, the split-brain patients, and heaps of psychology and neuroscience research have taught us this much. Although handedness is probably rooted somewhere in that duality, no one knows how handedness occurs, nor where precisely on the map of the brain it will show up, if at all.

But handedness may stem from the string of developmental instructions that makes us asymmetrical beings in the first place. Asymmetry encompasses much more than simply the preference for one hand over the other and uneven distribution of function within the brain. It's a whole-body phenomenon. True, we have roughly matching feet, ears, shoulders, and eyes, but look inside: heart slightly to the left, spleen on the right, lungs that aren't exactly the same—it would seem that our whole body structure is wildly out of whack.

Without much in-depth analysis, it's evident that a certain degree of asymmetry makes good evolutionary sense. It would be hard to run, for example, if the bottom of your body looked just like the top—one big, hard cranium crammed into an extra-wide sneaker. And if your eyes were randomly situated, that setup wouldn't be nearly as effective for vision as the layout to which we're more accustomed. Many studies have shown that organisms big and small have found evolutionary success with the help of asymmetrical anatomy. This is especially true for vertebrates like us, cashing in on survival benefits of lopsidedness as varied as superior movement of blood through the circulatory system and maximized space efficiency of abdomens crowded with organs.[3]

That lopsidedness in the body has proved advantageous is the easy part. Asymmetry of the brain is more complicated, and what might be more complicated still is determining the signals or mechanisms that drive lopsided development in the first place. Asymmetry's prevalence and importance does little to explain where it comes from. Scientists can say with relative confidence that genes are involved, but that only gets us so far. Understanding that something is genetic in origin is the equivalent of saying that the original blueprint for a cathedral has buttresses on it, and indeed anyone walking by the cathedral can see them. But knowledge of the blueprint does not explain how those buttresses are actually made. How nature makes a lopsided being requires the body, at the microscopic level, to comprehend left and right, or at least to understand it sufficiently enough to execute the construction of imbalanced anatomy.

In their earliest days, embryos appear to be symmetrical until something tips them off as to what is left and what is right, at which point they develop asymmetrically. How the cells of a developing embryo come to distinguish left from right or organize spatially in a way that distinguishes left from right has recently become a hot topic in molecular biology because it's fundamental to understanding the processes that shape us, from the smallest cells to the large muscles of the quadricep.

As it turns out, genetic research has revealed many of the steps in the sequence leading to asymmetrical organization within the body. These steps are often determined with the help of tests in which a gene is removed from laboratory-bred animals like mice and flies. Knocking out one of the genes, such as the one nicknamed "Sonic Hedgehog," messes with the normal chain of instructions and leads to sometimes subtle, sometimes drastic changes in anatomical development.

From the changes caused by a knockout test, scientists can link the deleted gene with a particular trait, whether the trait relates to skin pigment, the biochemistry of a particular protein, or possibly a behavior. A series of knockout tests years ago that led to altered layout of organs sent an instant buzz through the laterality research community. Knocking out a certain gene produced a population of mice whose hearts developed on the right 50 percent of the time instead of usually on the left as they normally do, just like in humans. Somehow, by knocking out this gene, bias to the left for heart location was eliminated.

This discovery eventually helped scientists find a genetic cause for a rare condition in which people are born with their internal organs flip-flopped, as if arranged through the looking glass by left-hander Lewis Carroll. Although fascinating, these cases did not reveal the mechanism or mechanisms in a developing embryo that *initially* trigger cellular "understanding" of left versus right. So how does the embryo "know" what is left and what is right? That's the question I've come to Tokyo hoping to answer.

About six years ago, Hirokawa and his team of researchers, using one of the world's most bad-ass microscopes, made a sizzling although accidental discovery that provides a likely scenario for how a developing body knows left from right. If the Japanese team is correct, it will have provided an essential piece to the larger mystery of asymmetry, including the brain asymmetry that probably underlies handedness.

Hirokawa's group had been studying a protein's role in the transport of nutrients and information within nerve cells. "Cells are like society," says Hirokawa, introducing what I can tell is a well-worn analogy. "Farmers and fishermen produce the food and transport it by various means to people in cities for consumption. Then around the city you have all sorts of manufacturing, and these things also need to be transported. Transportation is key for survival, and the same goes for all cellular function. Without mechanisms for transport, we die."

Investigating one particular protein within a developing organism, Hirokawa zoomed in and saw tiny, hair-like structures called monocilia. The monocilia were spinning, which surprised him because everyone up to that point had assumed that these monocilia, like others found elsewhere in our microscopic anatomy, only wave back and forth like seaweed swaying underwater. Hirokawa shows me a black and white video of these miniscule hairs in action, and they remind me of tiny sickle-shaped propellers. Here's the zinger: all of them were spinning from right to left. "When I saw this I thought it was fantastic," recalls Hirokawa. "I wanted to do a *banzai!*"

Using samples of these proteins taken from mice, Hirokawa's crew dropped fluorescent beads into the area where the propellers were spinning, not unlike tossing pieces of Styrofoam into the swirling eddy of a river. The tiny beads were all carried to the left by the clockwise-flowing current. Inside a young, symmetrical embryo, this flow of contents to one side of the protein would provide lopsidedness where once there was none. As one developmental biologist explained, "the accumulation of fluid and proteins on the left may then provide the bias required to break the initial embryonic symmetry. In other words, a feature of cellular architecture (the direction of rotation of [mono]cilia in the node) is translated into a left-right bias in embryonic development that effectively controls the way our internal organs develop."[4]

Next, Hirokawa wondered whether he could show that those tiny propellers play the role of sidedness conductors for organization of an entire body. He hypothesized that this right-to-left flow is the lead-off mechanism behind asymmetrical development. Accumulation of stuff on the left "informs" cells that the world they'll operate in has a left and a right side, that they'll need to develop accordingly, and that the direction of this propeller-induced flow is their guide to which side is which.[5] Toddlers have an "L" and an "R" painted on their sneakers, but cells and proteins need some other way to keep things straight.

To test the hypothesis, Hirokawa cooked up some interesting mouse embryos. By breeding mice with the gene for this specific protein knocked out of their genomes, Hirokawa could see how these mice developed differently compared to ordinary ones. The next click on his laptop brings up pinkish globs: mutant mouse embryos. Knocking out the gene resulted in mice that had a 50–50 chance of bodily asymmetry leaning left or leaning right.

Cranking up the microscope again, Hirokawa's team found that removing this particular protein had paralyzed the tiny hairs. Instead of rotating and creating a right-left current, the monocilia stood straight up and the fluorescent beads floated around aimlessly. That meant a 50–50 chance of material drifting to the left or to the right. If that current contains cellular blobs and globs of important information on how to develop asymmetrically, no longer would it be delivered exclusively to the left but rather randomly between left and right. Hirokawa had essentially crippled the mechanism conferring bias in one direction. Because mice bred without this protein had a 50–50 chance of having the heart on the left or the right, the implication was clear: somehow, the right-to-left flow created by the spinning monocilia triggered the left bias for location of the heart. Knock out or damage the gene governing this mechanism, and bias for a heart on the left is eliminated. It's not necessarily unusual for a single gene to determine the difference between, say, a perfectly healthy organism and a severe genetic disorder. Yet as someone obsessed with asymmetry, I find the role of this single gene, coding for this specialized spinning action within a particular protein, to be especially profound. Without it, half the human population would have reversed anatomical organization.

Hirokawa's tiny spinsters perform what may be the first step in the chain of uneven body building; the beginning of our unevenness. The theory is new but holding strong. Yale researcher Martina Brueckner initially doubted the role of these tiny monocilia because the imaging technology used by the Japanese was so sophisticated that it was difficult to replicate the research elsewhere. But then she finally saw the propellers with her own eyes. "Hirokawa is absolutely correct, the cilia do 'spin,' and it appears that at least in mice, and probably in fish also, directional spinning of node monocilia is the event that breaks embryonic bilateral symmetry."[6]

Interestingly, the theory for the role of these microscopic, one-armed pinwheels has also been effectively used to describe the human genetic disorder called Kartagener's syndrome. People with this condition are infertile and have chronic respiratory disease, and half of them have their internal organs arranged opposite the normal layout. Hirokawa shares an anecdote, though it may just be hearsay, of a burglar who was shot in the left side of the chest but survived because, as someone with Kartagener's, his heart was on the right.

At first, these three symptoms sound like a peculiar pot-pourri of unrelated conditions, but they're united by a common denominator. The infertility is caused by sperm that are paralyzed, unable to swim because sperm tails are essentially tiny hairs like monocilia. Likewise, the monocilia in the lungs don't work, rendering them incapable of effectively expelling unhealthy sputum, which leads to respiratory problems. The 50 percent chance of having organ layout reversed is an indicator of a random flip of a coin somewhere during development; think back to the paralyzed propellers and cellular material randomly floating about because of the absence of a clear right-to-left flow. All of this clinical evidence can be succinctly explained with the monocilia Hirokawa has found. The Kartagener's gene somehow impairs proper function of this tiny, hair-like component throughout the body—in sperm, in lungs, and in the transport proteins that initiate and possibly orchestrate asymmetrical development. This finding added further credibility to Hirokawa's model for how cells distinguish left from right.*

---

*Whether the monocilia necessarily dictate or signal asymmetrical development or just help the embryo recognize left versus right is unclear. Harvard biologists recently found that the neurochemical serotonin is present in vertebrate embryos before neuron cells form, and that it "plays a key role in determining where organs are positioned in the body during embryonic development." One possibility, suggests McManus, is that Hirokawa's cilia mechanism somehow amplifies an otherwise weak signal, but in this fast-paced and complicated field, little can be said with certainty. (See T. Fukumoto, I. P. Kema, and M. Levin, "Serotonin Signaling Is a Very Early Step in Patterning of the Left-Right Axis in Chick and Frog Embryos," Current Biology 15[May 10, 2005]:794–803.)

If this account seems distant from left-handedness, it isn't. As Hirokawa says: "We have found this surprising, upstream cause of left-right determination [during early development] that no one had imagined. We may meet the matter of hand preference in the future, by following these left-right studies, but now there remain many unknown gaps." What he means by "following" is tracking the steps from, say, the spinning monocilia to the transfer of information to the left side of cells, to the next three, five, 28 stages of development, on up to the particulars of brain asymmetry, where some difference may emerge between the brains of left-handers and right-handers. Filling all those gaps will take time.

Still, says Hirokawa, "definitely the mechanism that determines asymmetry of the body should connect to or cause asymmetry in the brain."[7] Getting from there to handedness requires more gap-closings, but then again, with people like Hirokawa busy playing with mutant mice and delving into the microscopic world of left versus right, maybe answers are closer than anyone thinks. In the spring of 2005, for example, scientists at Howard Hughes Medical Institute announced that they had found the role of a gene called LM04 to be significantly different in the left versus right side of the human brain. In mice, however, that difference was far more subtle, suggesting that LM04 plays a big part in making human brains so uneven.[8]

———◆———

During a recent discussion about handedness with a physics researcher at Stanford University named David Weld, I was introduced to a phenomenon in nature known as spontaneous symmetry breaking. It goes like this: Take a perfectly symmetrical Mexican sombrero and place a marble on top. Excluding such outside factors as friction, wind, or tiny manufacturing flaws—this is a *mathematically perfect* sombrero—try to predict what will happen to the marble. The laws of nature dictate that it will fall and settle in the circular valley of the hat. But the path it takes and the spot where it settles are fundamentally unpredictable. "The laws are symmetrical, but the system breaks the symmetry," says Weld. "It just kind of happens that way." Run the experiment again and again, and the same unpredictability persists.

Another example of this phenomenon can be found in magnets. The magnets sticking on your fridge are called ferromagnets, and at room temperature, they have a net magnetism, meaning their internal north and south poles are lined up and the magnets can stick to other magnets. The atoms of materials used to make ferromagnets (iron, nickel, and cobalt are three examples) "behave like tiny movable arrows that all like to line up pointing the same direction. In fact, these atoms are themselves like tiny bar magnets," adds Weld, each having north-south polarity, and the atoms are "happiest" if their north poles are pointing the same way as their neighbors' are. The needle of a compass points north because its magnetic north pole wants to line up with the magnetic north pole of the Earth.

Here's the cool part: Heat a magnet, and its atoms begin to spin, eliminating the ducks-in-a-row alignment that makes them magnetic. Cool them slowly, and that's when *it* will happen. Following on the coattails of one pioneering atom that settles leaning to either the north or the south (i.e., left or right), all the other atoms will settle oriented the same way, returning the material to a magnetic state. "The law only says the atoms 'like' to line up. But it doesn't determine left or right," says Weld. "The fact that that direction could be any direction, but ends up being a particular direction, is what is described as spontaneous symmetry breaking."

The magnets "have to line up" because an underlying, perhaps *the* underlying, law of the universe is symmetry, a law that explains such linchpin precepts as the conservation of energy. Closely following this heady stuff isn't crucial. What's thought-provoking, though, is that spontaneous symmetry breaking is a lopsided exception within the reality of our symmetry-driven universe, and that handedness, albeit with some imaginative threading, can link up with these fundamental, practically metaphysical aspects of our world.

Asymmetries in the human body—organ arrangement, cerebral function, and, more likely than not, handedness too—all have their evolutionary *raison d'être*, even if we haven't yet pinpointed them. We need to be asymmetrical, but the direction of those asymmetries, all other things being equal, is not unlike the Mexican hat potential. The direction of our asymmetry doesn't matter in terms of survival because the planet we operate on is symmetrical, or more precisely, is oblivious to the direction of our asymmetry. Fruit is just as likely to be plucked from a branch on the left as on the right; a child is just as likely to call for attention from the left as from the right; and a lion is just as likely to attack from the left as from the right. Humans normally have a heart a little to the left, but that's not because a heart to the left is inherently advantageous. Borrowing Weld's words, it just kind of happened that way.

In evolutionary terms, those tiny, clockwise-spinning monocilia, and the organisms they help to build, survived nature's hazards, and clockwise spin became the norm. But could the direction of that spinning—when it *first* evolved eons ago in our ancient ancestors—have been a spontaneous symmetry-breaking event? The movement of the propellers could have evolved to be a counterclockwise spin, initiating a cascade of developmental events putting the human heart on the right, the liver on the left, speech function usually in the right side of the brain, and handedness usually to the left hand. There's no way to know for sure, and maybe that small change would have doomed mammalian life. Yet it's also possible we would be no worse off for it.

"If you could run evolution all over again, it might choose to put the heart on the right and handedness on the left next time," muses Weld. It's a thought, I imagine, Lewis Carroll would have appreciated.

CHAPTER 11

Naisu BOru!

I'm so proud of the WALG flag.
To me you just can't go any higher.

———————

—Seventy-five-year-old Australian Doug Crosby,
president of the World Association of Left-Handed Golfers

I'm wearing the one and only golf shirt I own. It's a white polo embroidered with the red and black logo of the National Association of Left-Handed Golfers–Japan. After my visit with Nobutaka Hirokawa in Tokyo, I hopped the bullet train to Karuizawa, a small town in the foothills of the Japan Alps and home to some of the country's premier golf courses. This weekend, Karuizawa is hosting the NALG–Japan Tenth Anniversary Championships. Participants include 320 Japanese lefties, 28 players from Taiwan, the two senior Australians currently serving as president and secretary of the World Association of Left-Handed Golfers, and me.

Minutes before teeing off I try some stretches, thinking this might ease my anxiety, or at least help me feign steely nerves. It doesn't work. I can feel sweat collecting at the base of my back, which probably has something to do with the fact that I've only played four games of golf in my life. A swing resulting in zero ball contact is well within the realm of possibility.

Staying loose and relaxed is crucial, that much I know, but I have this creeping desire to hit a grand slam. You don't have to be a golfer—and God knows I'm not—to understand that some people play it safe, whereas other people, like "Lefty" Phil Mickelson, go for it. I want to be the type of guy who goes for it.

The gallery of onlookers swells in anticipation of the young foreigner's tee-off. Taking my stance, I draw a deep breath and try to empty my head. Instead, my cerebral stereo rings with a torrent of disparate instructions that have no collective meaning when it comes to muscle memory. Sportswriting legend George Plimpton spoke of a similar psychological phenomenon in *The Bogey Man*. Inside Plimpton's head a crew of Japanese World War II navy admirals shouted commands much like the ones I'm hearing now: rock back; arms straight; stay low; elbows in; pause at the top; explode with the hips; head down; and worst of all, just relax.

As if possessed by the spirit of a true golfer, I miraculously send the ball sailing straight down the fairway. Everyone claps, and I can only laugh in disbelief. In the photograph someone handed me at the end of the tournament, I'm at the apex of my opening drive, arms curling over my right shoulder, hips twisted, a wrinkled expression on my face. I'm happy with the photo, though. I didn't whiff on that pressure-packed first shot, and I think I know why.

I've been riding a uniquely Southpaw sort of high. "Kind of bizarre, all those lefties in the same place," said my younger brother, Dan, when I first told him about the tournament.

"Like a gathering of deformed people or a four-leaf clover patch." The idea of an all-lefties sporting event may strike some as peculiar. But for me, the World Association of Left-Handed Golfers, and this event put on by the Japanese chapter, are like a homecoming. Hundreds of lefties, fresh off the links, sharing their experiences as left-handers in a right-handed world—this is where I belong. These people are my brethren.

———•◆•———

Walking through the arrivals lobby at Narita International Airport, I greet a 5′5″, bespectacled Japanese man with a sign that says: "Dave." Tsutomu Waki is a dentist; vice-president of the National Association of Left-Handed Golfers–Japan; and, I will quickly learn, instrumental in organizing this year's annual championship tournament. A veteran of the lefty golf circuit, Waki and his wife Mie have traveled to events in places as faraway as Spain, Canada, and New Zealand.

While we sit in an airport Starbucks waiting for the Australians to arrive, I ask Waki what the rule is for tournament qualification, how organizers distinguish between South-paws worthy of a spot in the event versus, say, mixed-handed posers. I expect to hear something about the Edinburgh Handedness Inventory or maybe dynamic dominance. "You have to swing from the left side of the ball," says Waki. "That's all."

In terms of the popular notion of lefty identity, sports are probably more important than nuances of neuropsychology recognizable only to academic researchers. In some games it's true: lefties have an edge. Andrew Kerr knew this all too well, although fencing in the Borderlands was no game. Lefty batters are a step closer to first base, and a left-handed relief pitcher will always have a job because of that special curve. A football team is constructed around a right-handed quarterback, making the left tackle a marquee lineman because he's charged with protecting the quarterback's blind side against the other team's pass rush. A lefty quarterback like Steve Young confuses a football roster, even though he also provides a team with a distinct advantage because lefties are unusual. On the other hand, playing polo left-handed is forbidden because someone could get cracked in the head with a mallet. Boxing offers similar advantages as tennis and fencing, and then there are all those other sports that involve facing off against someone with a nonlethal weapon (squash, ping-pong, badminton, etc.). Left-handed tennis players, as mentioned earlier, are less familiar to their opponents, causing confusion over which side will bear the forehand versus the backhand, and a lefty's ad-court serve can be lethally out of reach.

From a distance, the game of tennis looks balanced: the ball, court, racket—all perfectly symmetrical. Yet I have a theory that lefties possess an additional advantage—beyond the edge of the unfamiliar—because of the way the game is scored. Tennis matches, like ping-pong and volleyball contests, require players to win by two points. That is, if the score is even at deuce (40–40), someone needs to win two points in a row to win a game. Pros may disagree with the following statement, and their skill often belies such simple classification, but common tennis logic has it that righties have an advantage serving to the server's left, whereas lefties have an advantage serving to the right, also known as the ad court ("ad" for advantage, though no pun intended). From their respective stronger sides, players can hit the ball at an angle that makes it harder for an opponent to successfully return it back over the net.

Potentially game-winning points, with the exception of points played at 40–15 (tennis jargon for 3–1), are always played from the ad court, a.k.a left-handers' strong side. At 40–0, 40–30, and, perhaps most significantly, all ad points, Southpaws get to serve for the game from their preferred side. True, to get to the game-winning point when the score is tied, they have to serve to the deuce or left side of the court and win the point, but I'm still curious if there's something legitimate going on here. McEnroe, Navratilova, Connors, Ivanisevic, Laver, Seles, Vilas, Muster, Leconte, Woodforde, Gomez, Nadal, and many other left-handers fill the ranks of the game's greatest players. It turns out, Marian Annett and some other researchers actually crunched data to see if lefties are overly represented in the highest levels of tennis. The result: Annett thinks so, others do not. Nevertheless, my own little theory about the game being quietly rigged in favor of left-handers could be true. If that's the case, though, an explanation for why lefties *aren't* overly represented at the top of tennis is needed, leading to the possibility that right-handers have some other sort of edge that helps them overcome the game's structural bias that favors left-handers.

Baseball is also worthy of some extra attention because of a left/right asymmetry subtler than the more well-known differences of stance on one side of the plate, curveballs, and shorter distance to first base. A few years ago, I contacted a University of California at Berkeley professor of psychology named Richard Ivry for a story on whether being a natural left-hander gives San Francisco Giants slugger Barry Bonds an additional edge when it comes to hitting home runs. This was in 2001, Bonds's blockbuster, 73 home run year, and other, performance-enhancing influences had not yet made headlines.

Ivry had examined a possible connection between handedness and hitting. When compared to right-handers who have learned to hit from the left side of the plate, true lefties, according to Ivry's work, have an advantage when it comes to power hitting. He and a colleague analyzed the batting history of 3,300 players. More than 1,000 of these players batted from the left side of the plate, although only a small fraction of them were natural lefties. As is common in baseball, many righties learn to hit from the left side of the plate so they can be a step closer to first base and get a slightly longer look at the ball coming in from righty pitchers.

Although many people talk about left or right hand preference, Ivry's research is another reminder of the fact that humans perform most functions bimanually, in other words, with both hands. "The literature is dominated by left versus right, whereas we usually use the two hands together in different ways," he says.[1] Playing piano, chopping wood, sweeping, swinging a baseball bat—you get the idea.

When using both hands on a tool, the grip changes depending on the task. For a power grip used to swing an axe or a bat, the dominant hand is usually atop the nondominant hand. With the precision grip, however, like when slicing vegetables, the dominant hand is placed further down on the implement for better control of the active end of the tool. For natural lefties standing in the batter's box, the dominant hand is where one would expect for a power grip, higher up on the bat, whereas for righties who've learned to hit from the left side of the plate, the dominant hand is in the lower position, or what researchers call the precision grip.

In the home runs study, Ivry analyzed the hand preference and batting statistics of the players and confirmed the hypothesis: natural lefties have statistically more home runs but also more strike outs and less control. Bonds's unbelievable 73 homeruns and only 49 singles, though a sole data set, make a primo case in point. When asked about his performance, Bonds often insisted that he wasn't swinging for the fences, just hitting the way he knew how. That explanation, says Ivry, fits well with the predictions for how the body works.

In golf, however, the role of handedness is less apparent. It's not a game played directly against an opponent in the combat sense, only in the scorecard sense. Nor is golf a game in which left-handers have a strategic or mechanical advantage, with two possible exceptions. First, I've been told that lefties who learn to play golf right-handed have an advantage on the putting green. When putting, the lead or front arm needs to stay rigid and straight, and for lefties who putt righty, that lead arm is the left one and thus, presumably, will more accurately obey motor instructions from the golfer's brain.

Secondly, golf courses, usually designed by right-handers, may have a couple of holes laid out in a way intended to challenge most golfers, who are righties, and these holes end up to be a little easier for lefties. The opposite is true too, however, with nonobstacles for righties obscuring shots for lefties, so any such differences generally cancel themselves out. Besides, subtleties of course design really only matter at the highest levels of golf, for that population of alien creatures who have uncanny accuracy when hitting a golf ball. For the rest of us, lateral biases of course design don't really matter.

But lefties are at a disadvantage in golf when it comes to gear. At first I thought this was one of those whiny, outdated complaints, irrelevant in the age of equality and materialism when no one group is left out because there is money to be extracted from every niche population. Left-handers can obviously obtain proper equipment for whatever sport. But left-handed amateurs and weekend golfers have far fewer options to try out when they walk into a store. Before the big event in Karuizawa, I wandered into a golf store in Tokyo's Ginza ward, one of the planet's most bustling, overpriced, and essentially insane epicenters of consumerism. The clerk walked me to the farthest possible corner of the store and spread his arms about half his total wingspan to indicate that this section encompassed the entire, pathetic selection of lefty gear. Then he apologized profusely.

Despite troubles with gear, some lefty golfers have made it to the top. The most famous are probably, and in this order: American Phil Mickelson, Canadian Mike Weir, and New Zealander Bob Charles. According to the Royal Canadian Golf Association, 25–30 percent of Canadian golfers play left-handed, the highest percentage anywhere, probably because many righties prefer playing hockey with the left hand lower on the stick, and this same posture is adopted for swinging a golf club. As for golf's lefty elite, I don't think being left-handed matters much to them— Mickelson, for example, is a righty who only plays golf left-handed. If it did matter, one would think that by now they would have shown up at, or at least sent a Christmas card to, the Association of Left-Handed Golfers in their respective countries.

To show my respect for the Southpaw golf community, I decided to play. But to prepare for the tournament, I had to learn the game quickly. That meant: a) a golf lesson one afternoon in Scottsdale, Arizona; b) buying two books: *Bob Charles' Guide to Left-Handed Golf* and George Plimpton's *The Bogey Man*, about Plimpton's frustrating attempt to play alongside the pros; c) recruiting my brother, Dan, a golf enthusiast and certified ESPN addict, to play Mr. Miagi to my "Karate Kid" for one week; d) consulting a well-established golf writer about tournament protocol and any additional advice. His words weren't exactly gentle.

"You've never played? And this event is in what, five weeks?"

"Correct."

"You need to find a course and get out there every day between now and when you leave for Japan. Find a pro too. Explain your situation and see how many lessons you can get. Try to have one at least once a week. Tell him you just need to be able to fake it."

"OK," I say, but this is a white lie because I don't have the time nor the money for golf lessons.

His final warning is rather severe: "You don't want to be the fat, out-of-shape guy on a hiking trip who's holding everyone up. That's what's going to happen if you don't get out there and practice."

This is a good point. Up to now I'd been thinking of golf in terms of individual performance, ignoring the reality of a group outing in which four people move through the course with some semblance of a steady pace. My status as a neo-phyte golfer might be so overwhelmingly embarrassing that I'll be forced to fall on my club *harakiri*-style.

In light of the impossibility of legitimate skill development, I was determined to mask my ineptitude by at least looking the part. Although the phone call with Nike's sponsorship and marketing whiz ended abruptly, the woman said something to the effect of: "So let me get this straight. You've barely ever played golf, which means you're likely going to play badly, maybe even come in last. Why would we want you wearing Nike?" I acquiesced that based on a rigid, humorless understanding of "brand image," her logic was half-decent, but I still submitted my formal written request.

I never heard back from Nike. Stiffed without so much as a rejection letter, I took off for Japan by my lonesome, carrying $40 golf shoes bought on clearance, a plastic supermarket bag with a handful of balls and tees, and a used glove.

On the plane I kicked back with Plimpton and read about a golfer from the 1950s named Lefty Stackhouse, famous for venting frustration by physically abusing himself with kicks to his own shin, smacks to his own head, and even whacks against a tree with his own apparently disobedient arm. Coincidentally, Baltimore Orioles legend Lefty Grove had similar explosive tendencies. I realized quickly, however, that if I was going to fit in at all with the other golfers in Japan, such tantrums would be out of the question.

The Japanese are notoriously crazy about golf, paying stratospheric greens and club membership fees, obsessing over equipment, even buying hole-in-one insurance to protect against the financial burden of having to lavish golf partners with gifts, as is customary should one be unfortunate enough to sink a hole in one. There are probably a couple of dusty dissertations out there on the subject of the Japanese and golf, exploring exactly how the Japanese culture is so mystically compatible with the sport. My guess? It's some kind of connection between the "all life is suffering" theme of Buddhism and golf's inherent suffering.

After two years of living in Japan, I knew proper decorum would be essential. I have great respect for the culture's premium on politeness and manners, but not knowing the code of conduct can be disconcerting. On the upside, the Japanese are so polite and careful to shield true emotions that were I to disrupt the tournament disastrously, it's doubtful anyone would voice contempt until I was well on my way back to the United States.

Japan also has an interesting relationship to left-handedness. As in other parts of the world, use of the left hand has been severely looked down upon throughout Japanese history. Whereas countries such as the United States mostly loosened up about children writing and eating with the left hand in the last 30 to 40 years, in places like Japan and China that loosening of attitudes has been more recent, perhaps just in the past 10 to 15 years. Most of the participants at the NALG–Japan event, for example, are middle-aged or older, and only a tiny fraction of them, as far as I could tell during the banquet and award ceremony, use chopsticks with the left hand. Most have been taught (read: forced) to eat with the right hand.

The rise to equality for lefties in many parts of Asia remains incomplete, at least according to people I got to know in Japan in the late 1990s. Discussing the matter over drinks with a journalist friend in Tokyo whose wife is left-handed, he pointed out that this persisting prejudice is in part because pressure to conform is such a powerful force in Japanese culture. That may explain why some studies into the demographics of left-handedness and its distribution around the world were confused by data out of countries like Japan, where people were even more likely to cloak or lie about hand preference. One survey of handedness in Japan came back reporting that less than 2 percent of the entire population was left-handed.[2] The history of lefty denial and oppression, I felt, made it that much more imperative for me to join my Southpaw comrades on the links.

———•◆•———

By the time I arrive in Karuizawa I'm too late to join the pretournament practice round, but I have plenty of time to hit the driving range, where I'm informed that left-handers are quarantined to the far right side of the sweeping, crescent-shaped range made up of 100 generously sized practice spaces. The idea, I imagine, is to prevent back-to-back golfers, one lefty and one righty, from cracking each other's skulls with a swing. It's technically a voluntary isolation, but it would be more of a hassle than it's worth to complain, so I trek out to the very last slot.

My strokes are troubling, to say the least. Perhaps it's the *sake* from last night or the particulate matter in the air from a nearby volcano that's been erupting over the past few weeks. Whatever the cause, I'm Sir Shankalot. To my right sits a maintenance shed and a small stand of pine trees. When I skunk one ball and send it sailing into the pines, it bounces off one of the trunks and dribbles back into the feet of an old guy, also a lefty, working on his drives just a few slots away from me.

The next morning I put on my new NALG–Japan embroidered shirt and at the hotel gift shop I buy an Aquarius sports drink for an added boost. According to the English-language description on the bottle, it "enables quick recovery for your parched body and spirit by adjusted osmotic pressure, and its five ingredients support to keep you going." The Aquarius must have done the trick because when I finally tee off at 9:40 A.M., I crush the ball. The miracle shot is straight and far, and I'm ecstatic.

My group for the day includes Nakajima and Inoue, both from the northern prefecture of Yamagata, and a quiet guy from Tokyo named Taguchi. Inoue has a potbelly, thick glasses, and smokes a cigarette between—and sometimes during—almost every hole. After I tee off, Nakajima says the small crowd gathered to watch me is now making *him* terribly nervous. I watch him tee off, but I'm so intoxicated with relief about my own successful drive that the product of his swing doesn't even register. If the first hole is any measure of what's ahead, the day will not just be memorable, it will be miraculous: I make par—my first ever.

On the next hole I whiff on my second shot. The guys, almost in unison, tell me not to worry and insist I do it over. I refuse their charity. Six strokes later, the hole is finished, and even though I screw up a good handful of shots over the next seven holes, for the most part I keep pace. The few times I do manage a decent shot, the guys cheer wildly. "Naisu **SH**o!" they call out from the fairway, the Japanese version of the English word, "nice," combined with "sho," the Japanglish version of "shot." Other useful permutations of this compliment include "Naisu **BO**ru!" for "Nice ball!" and for nice touch with a chip or a putt, "Naisu **TA**chi!"

I complete the front nine with a score of 55. For golf afi-cionados seeking more detail, I have two bogeys accompa-nying the still-unbelievable par, and my worst score for a hole is 8 (twice). Short chips remain by far my worst en-emy, some of them sailing from one side of the green over to the other, or worse.

On the back nine, things fall apart. The charade cannot hold. I start with a drive that goes *maybe* 35 yards, stopping a foot from a pond, and that isn't even my worst shot of the afternoon. I finish the day with a 126. The score is a bum-mer considering my success on the front nine, but at least I rarely held up the group behind us. As one player put it: "You're not the last finisher. Another player has 126."

During the evening banquet and auction, the huge dinner hall at the hotel is filled with lefty golfers, their spouses, and a 60-yard-long buffet spread staffed by upwards of 20 chefs with tall, white hats. Visiting lefty-golf dignitaries give short speeches, followed by a welcome address from Tetsuharu Kawakami, president of NALG–Japan and a former baseball star who's as famous in Japan as Joe DiMaggio is in the United States. At one point the emcee welcomes each group from the different areas of Japan, and when their respective lefty golf association is called out—Hokkaido, Kyushu, Shikoku—all those representatives jump from their seats and cheer. The Taiwanese group is especially loud. Then I hear: "Furom za Yunaiteto Stayyto, miss-ta Debido Uoruman-sama." It takes me a moment to realize this means me. With everyone clapping, I sheepishly stand, give a half-assed queen's wave, then quickly sit down.

———•◆•———

On Day 2 things really get away from me. Teeing off this time on the Higashi Iriyama course, I chunk out, as in totally miss the ball and take a clump out of the turf. Trying again, this time I send the ball sailing toward the next hole to the left, on a beeline for a cart and a group of golfers. In unison, the guys in my group and all those watching yell out the Japanese version of "fore!" which is "fah!" though it sounds more like a squealing, panicky version of 'baaaahhhh!' as if warning against an incoming sheep-shaped meteorite.

The first two holes are pure mortification, resulting in scores of 12 and 15 respectively, although the 15 deserves an asterisk because one of the guys in my foursome, thinking I couldn't see him up by the green, used his putter to nudge my ball out of a bunker. One might argue that this was done simply out of impatience, but I believe it was a gesture of saintly generosity. Even our 60-ish caddie wants to help me climb out of the darkness of my own gloom. From beneath a huge visor that looks like those plastic cones that injured dogs have to wear, she suggests I relax more with my shoulders, step closer to the ball, shift my stance a little to the left, and—painfully reminiscent of my mother's advice back in the days of little league—"keep your eye on the ball."

One of the guys in my foursome the first day, Taguchi, had told me that I put too much left-arm power into my swing, which makes sense because many of my shots were indicative of someone who fails to execute one of golf's golden rules:

the straight, strong lead arm. For Southpaws, that means the right arm, and when I wake up the next morning with a sore left shoulder, I remember Taguchi's input. This error of technique is annoying because my downfall at arguably the biggest all-lefties event of my life is due in part to an inability to properly manipulate my *right* arm. Robert Sainburg, the coordination guy at Penn State, comes to mind. Was my right-arm-left-brain system shirking its responsibility as the stabilizer? Maybe Toledo's Stephen Christman should do a study on whether mixed-handed people are better golfers. As a strong left-hander, I start to wonder whether my destiny lies in a more one-arm-centric sport like bowling.

At the end of the day, after I've tabulated my score of 153, two players heartily shake my hand and tell me it was a good experience for them to play with me. "We were nervous to have a white guy in our group because whenever we watch guys that look like you play on television, they're all really good golfers. Now we know better."

Packing up my shoes back in the clubhouse, I recall Plimpton's words about how golf lacks the camaraderie of other sports and remains a more private enterprise. Although true in a sense and probably more true at the professional level, I can't say I agree as far as WALG goes. This whole weekend is built on a premise of a particular, if not peculiar, commonality that catalyzes friendships. Despite my awful performance, I feel like I've been accepted and welcomed into this club, which is good because I'm the worst golfer these people have ever seen.

I used to think golf was asinine: just a lot of rich people walking, looking for little pock-marked balls over ecologically ransacked terrain. But what I failed to understand is that golf, at least at my level, has little to do with the ball and less to do with the course and far more to do with the people you play with. Hiking the Appalachian Trail, writer Bill Bryson was similarly struck when he realized hiking has less to do with solitude and more to do with personalities encountered along the way. With golf, if you can find your people, you can find a way to like this game. For me, those people are the members of the World Association of Left-Handed Golfers.

But what I'd really come to Karuizawa looking for was an essential truth about left-handedness. During the inaugural dinner with baseball legend Kawakami, I'd asked him about matters of left and right. He gave the usual answers, about the shortage of lefty golf gear, and the baseball hitter's advantage of being closer to first base, before pausing to look down at his hands in his lap. "I believe there is something genius in lefties. I don't know what that something is . . . maybe it has to do with being artistic." Then he adds that he practices Zen, bringing on a moment saturated with profundity potential: the slightly drunk, aging Japanese baseball god, delivering what I expect to be a nugget of priceless wisdom, and quite possibly the key that will finally unlock the gates of Southpaw nirvana. Might there be a connection between left-handedness and, say, Zen enlightenment?

"No," he says. "Nor is there any difference between left- and right-handed people. Not as I see it."

What? That can't be right.

CHAPTER 12

A Parent's
Guide to Handedness

The use of the right hand in preference to
the left must be regarded as a general
characteristic of the family of man.[1]

—*Andrew Buchanan*, Proceedings of the
Philosophical Society of Glasgow, *1860–1864*

I would enthusiastically encourage all
left-handed children, and adults for that matter,
to pursue their dreams with hope and confidence.[2]

—*Jane M. Healey*, Loving Lefties: How to Raise
Your Left-Handed Child in a Right-Handed World

My sister Sarah is about to kill me. For co-opting her
four-year-old to serve as a research guinea pig, I probably deserve it. Whether this visit to a child neuropsychologist ultimately inflicts real damage to little Sam's psyche or just convinces his mother that it could have, the end result will likely be the same: severed relations with Uncle Dave.

Southpaw neuropsychologist Jane M. Healey, an expert on child psychology and handedness, once worked alongside such laterality bigwigs as Harvard's Norman Geschwind. Unfortunately, she won't do any sort of evaluation of me, explaining that adults are outside her area of expertise. When I offer to spend the $200, hour-long session pretending to be a six-year-old, she still declines. Needing a child and not having one of my own, I decide to borrow Sam. On a summer morning, Sarah, Sam, and I cruise up the New Jersey Turnpike to Healey's office in Ridgewood. For Sam, the trip is billed as a visit to meet Uncle Dave's friend, Jane. For me, the goal is to gain insight into Sam's yet-to-be-determined hand preference and learn about handedness in children more generally.

Most everyone who has ever been a parent, aunt, uncle, or grandparent wants to know when kids reveal whether they're right- or left-handed. Is there an age when they should be taking a side? As adults, do our lateral biases transmit to or somehow bias children's handedness behavior? Overt actions like scolding a child for using the left hand will, as they have for millennia, influence the child's long-term handedness tendencies. But do children also copy parents or siblings with tasks like writing and eating? If a certain cramped kitchen layout means a child in a highchair usually receives food on her right side, will that have some kind of long-term effect?

I try not to bias Sam's hand preference because it would infuriate Sarah, although that doesn't keep me from inwardly celebrating every time I see him swing a bat or scoop cereal with his left hand, as if having a left-handed nephew might miraculously boost the Southpaw minority. Unlikely at best, yet still, I cross my fingers and hope this nephew, who everyone says looks like me, is also a Southpaw.[3]

The four of us are in Healey's office, three adults eyeing Sam's hands as he stands by a table and colors on a large pad. "All right, Sam," says Healey, indicating that drawing time is over. "Come here. OK. Close your eyes." Healey's trying to get Sam's attention, but he mostly ignores her. Eventually, he puts down the colored pencils, then starts playing some form of modified peek-a-boo. Sarah, seated behind him on Healey's floral print couch next to a phrenology bust, tries some redirecting.

"Are you peeking?" she says, playing along.

Sam peeks and giggles. Sarah says Jane has a fun game to play.

Healey, trying again: "Close your eyes. Now, I'm going to give you this color [marker]. Close your eyes. Put your hands next to your body. Oh good, put them behind your back. OK. Now when I say go, you're going to grab this marker and make a letter on the page, or just scribble. Are you ready? OK. Ready? Here it is—go grab it!"

Sam, eyes closed, reaches out with both hands simultaneously, taking the marker as if it were a samurai sword. He then proceeds, with his right hand, to draw a giant "B," although the significance of his hand choice at this instant is of little to no consequence, considering the dual-hand grab and how much hand switching he's been doing during the past ten minutes, to say nothing of the past ten months. What was supposed to happen was a one-handed grab, which can be a clue, says Healey, to underlying hand preference. Sarah and I try not to crack up at the botched experiment, but we've never been good at concealing laughter. Sam picks up the vibe and jumps in.

"I grabbed it!" he says mischievously.

Healey suggests he resume coloring. Over her shoulder is a stuffed Kermit the Frog hanging off a bookshelf next to a sign reading: "Everyone's born right-handed. Only the greatest can overcome it!" In a few minutes, Sarah takes Sam to the bathroom. Things are off to an awkward start.

When they return, Healey asks Sarah how old Sam is and whether he's started school. "He's in pre-K? OK, in pre-K he should make a decision [about left- versus right-hand writing] by the end of the year. That would be the best, the wisest thing to do. The reason for that is so that he can develop the motor programs for the symbols, drawing, shapes—what they call prewriting." This is the cognitive stuff that leads to letters and then writing, and Healey wants to make sure children are well positioned to develop these critical skills as smoothly as possible.

Sam starts drawing his favorite word, and Healey gestures toward the paper and Sam's cubist rendition of the letters M-O-M-M-Y. "What Sam's showing us here is that his system is already developing. The fine motor system is moving very quickly. . . . In other words, you better start moving because this is a natural occurrence, a development here. Most boys his age are not doing what he just did in front of me. I figured 'oh, he's got another year, don't even think about it.' But he starts writing letters?! And not only that, little letters."

Where or what Sarah is supposed to "start moving" isn't clear, but later Healey clarifies what my sister and I mistook for some kind of dire message. A healthy child will almost always sort out hand preference on his own and completely naturally. But Healey advises that by the time a child reaches kindergarten, parents should gently encourage writing practice with either the left or the right hand. "That is because the motor programs are laid down on one side of the brain when you use one hand, and on the other side of the brain when you use the other hand." At the early stages of this wiring process, children can run into confusion if they keep switching hands. She's quick to emphasize, however, that the idea of helping children opt for one hand over the other only applies to writing, and only when children reach kindergarten. Otherwise, mixed-handedness, whether in a 3-year-old or a 30-year-old, is normal and not known to cause motor or cognitive problems. On the contrary, as Stephen Christman and many others have illustrated, it may in fact have certain advantages.

Parents who curiously observe their children's hand preference tendencies are in good company. Charles Darwin took careful notes during the early years of his son William's development, watching and wondering when the boy would demonstrate whether he was left- or right-handed.[4] Even though William turned out to be a Southpaw, it took many years for definitive handedness to emerge. That's because young children are like scientists, busy experimenting, in this case with how their different appendages operate in the world. Doodling and eating are not fine motor skills requiring premium dexterity, which is why many babies and toddlers, under the influence of rapidly developing brains, switch between using the left and right hands, often masking underlying handedness and leading parents to conclude falsely that their children are ambidextrous. This is a common error among people who associate ambidextrousness with high intellect, as if it were some kind of verification that the Mozart CDs, trilingual nanny, and baby yoga classes were paying off.

It's tempting to say that young children "develop" hand preference, but "demonstrate" is the correct word. Under the prevailing genetic model, environment and culture can and certainly do influence lateral behaviors, but true handedness, loaded term that it is, is believed to be wired within each person's brain before birth. It's just not expressed or observable in infants or toddlers until they begin carrying out fine motor skills, especially writing. That means studying theories of the origins of handedness or even the biochemical pathways that, as Nobutaka Hirokawa suggests, lead to asymmetrical development can't tell us anything about when handedness is detectable in young people. With infants as with chimpanzees, you can't watch them take notes or ask them to fill out questionnaires.

Sam is in every sense a normal child in that he often switches hands for tasks like drawing, brushing his teeth, eating, and picking his nose. But as kids try to master fine motor coordination for writing, their brains busily building new connections and laying down neurological foundations for this skill, they will likely have an easier time of things, says Healey, with a gradual focus on one hand or the other. Eventually, for children who are 4, 5, 6 years of age, too much ping-ponging between the left and right hands in the classroom might slow them as they learn to write. Unless a child is really struggling, however, parents would do best to employ a chilled-out attitude because more often than not the best tactic is to let handedness blossom on its own and at its own pace. If it's not doing so by age seven or eight, call Uncle Dave's friend Jane.

Before children begin to tackle writing, there's zero reason for parents to be concerned about handedness, aside from curiosity. In cultures where left-handedness is chastised, I can see where parents might get hyped-up about hand usage, but here, in the enlightened USA? I had assumed, perhaps foolishly, that encouraging kids to become naturally comfortable with one hand or the other was sort of a no-brainer. Not true, says Healey. She's amazed by the number of parents who still worry if their child is left-handed and ask how that might negatively impact the child's education.

Healey also asks about Sam's family history of left-handedness. Sarah says his grandmother on his father's side is probably left-handed, but she was forced to switch and write with her right hand when she was in grade school. And of course, there's his uncle. Healey nods. "All right, so he has about a 15- to 20-percent chance of being left-handed. Probably 1 or 2 percent more because he's a boy."

"And how are those chances affected by this discussion?" asks Sarah, faking a laugh. When she glances in my direction, the sibling telepathy message pops up on my cerebral monitor: Dave, this is not as fun as you'd advertised.

A few minutes later, Healey tries to get Sam to play along with a different activity, but Sam's just a little too young for the "games" used to study handedness. Frustrated with us for repeatedly urging him to try the game with one hand, he finally says: "Everyone can do their own hand," as in, each unto their own, so back off, which may be the smartest thing I've heard all day.

As for Sarah's influence on Sam's handedness, she's careful not to steer him one way or the other. She passes him pens straight on instead of to one hand, never suggests he

clockwise, whereas lefties more often turn counterclockwise. And according to Bulgarian scientists, most people, especially right-handers, are more likely to opt for a seat on the right side of a movie theater.[10]

Humans, like rats, also have a biochemical imbalance in the brain stem. McManus makes the connection to handedness like this: Place a beer just out of arm's reach and then pick it up. "Think carefully about the muscles of the shoulders and upper trunk as you do it, and you'll find that as the arm reaches out so the upper part of the body also turns. Hand preference might well be something to do with primitive turning tendencies, although quite how is not yet clear."[11] In other words, if people have this natural inclination to turn one way or the other, maybe hand preference is just a derivative of this embedded turning bias.

The truth is that a lot of this stuff remains unclear. Returning to the subject of children, even the age when handedness shows up varies depending on whom you ask, with some sources saying by age 1 or 2, others saying 3, 4, or older. "My best reading is that maybe by 10–11 months of age, you're starting to get a lot of indicators about direction," says Michigan State University's Lauren Harris, whereas McManus says "handedness of children typically only becomes apparent in their second year."[12] However, most experts are quick to agree that older children who haven't yet demonstrated preferences are not behind in their cognitive or motor development in any significant way. And, at least in my view, the mixed-handed tendency of a child like Sam is a valuable reminder that a large proportion of people are destined to be mixed-handed anyway and thus may never reveal a definitive leaning to the left or right.

Yet as is so often the case with left-handers, one additional ingredient is worth mixing into this confusing goulash: in left hand–preferring infants and young children, preference fluctuations are more dramatic. That is, with a large enough group of two-year-olds, more fluctuations in hand preference will show up among the left hand–leaning toddlers than among the right-preferring ones. "For some reason, the developmental trajectory is more stable in right-handers than in left-handers," says Harris. It's the kind of footnote-style distinction that will become pivotal in the final stretches of my journey.

CHAPTER 13

All-Star

"Finding the right hand is my job," Dr. Zajac said.
"It's a left hand," Wallingford reminded him.
"Of course it is! I mean the right donor."[1]

—*John Irving*, The Fourth Hand

Now a surgeon should be youthful or at any
rate nearer youth than age; with a strong and
steady hand that never trembles, and ready
to use the left hand as well as the right; with vision
sharp and clear and spirit undaunted.[2]

—*Celsus*

John Evans sips black currant iced tea through a straw,
then leans across the table. With the fork sticking out of
the Velcro strap wrapped around his hand, he scoops another bite of salad and ferries it to his mouth. He wears a yellow and gold ring, a tiger's eye cameo like the one his father
used to wear. I get confused trying to determine if the ring's
on his fourth or second finger. In a way, the answer is both.

Such is the paradoxical handedness of the coolest Southpaw I've ever met. Although with his left hand attached to his right arm, Evans isn't technically a left-hander. Or is he?

When he laughs, Evans leans his bald head far to the left or right. On this particular day, he sometimes leans far enough to the right that his head rests against the pale yellow wall of Pastabilities Italian restaurant in downtown Decatur, Illinois. Eventually, Evans tells me his story. "You could say it like: 'I got hit by a train. I lost my arm. Here I am.'" You could say it like that, but that doesn't do justice to the ordeal or to the man.

On a late summer evening ten years ago, Evans was walking from the gas station near Water Street and the Garver's Feed Store just 12 blocks from here, where he'd bought a soda. Heading toward the rail tracks that transect the town, he saw a train's lights in the distance but thought he could easily make it across well before the oncoming train arrived. He wasn't drinking.

As Evans remembers it, his foot got stuck between the inner and outer portions of the rail. "I tried jerking my whole body back and forth. It felt like it was getting looser, and I think it was, but not enough. I remember lights and a whistle. Then nothing." Some people speculate that Evans, an epileptic, had a seizure just as he was crossing the tracks, but no one can know for sure. About 20 minutes later, "they found my body in one spot, and my arm I-don't-know-how-many yards away," he says, swinging his one arm in the air to emphasize distance. Although Evans can't remember anything between the whistle of the 122-car freight train and being wheeled through a hospital corridor many hours later, the detective on the scene reported that when he approached a body by the tracks, Evans sat up like a rocket, looked down at his grue-some disfigurement, and shouted at the man to shoot him.

Dr. Richard Brown thought it was a crank call. A special-ist with Southern Illinois University's Institute of Plastic and Reconstructive Surgery, Brown had just completed an eight-hour shift at the Memorial Medical Center in Spring-field and figured some cheeky medical student had called in the rare case of a double amputee. "But that double amputee was real," says Evans. When Evans first arrived, the doctors could peer into the opening where his left arm once was, all the way into his chest cavity to his beating heart. Whereas his right hand was mutilated, the left hand at the end of his lost left arm remained intact. In a 12-hour procedure, Brown and colleagues closed up Evans's left side, carefully salvaged the left hand from the orphaned arm that paramedics had thrown on ice in the ambulance, and attached it to Evans's right wrist.

Back in his one-bedroom apartment, Evans shows me photographs from the surgery, enclosed carefully within the thick album of press clippings that a friend put together for him. In the medical photographs, the mangled right hand lies on a sterile blue sheet, more Hollywood than human. Next to it is the left arm, bright red and meaty at the upper segment and shoulder, peacefully unaffected from the bicep down to the fingertips.

Brown decided almost immediately to attempt the transfer surgery, only the second ever in the United States. To pull off the switch, he and his team crisscrossed the most critical ten-dons and nerves to provide Evans with as much mobility as possible. The intricate weaving meant that to move his thumb, Evans wouldn't have to think about moving his pinky,

and vice versa. Still, such movements took months of practice and therapy.

"My doctor doesn't know his right from his left, and I can
prove it!" Evans is always teasing, which includes recount-
ing episodes in which he's teasing other people, usually doctors, nurses, reporters, hotel receptionists, waiters, and most
of all himself: "I can play with my food and get away with
it," he says, recalling a time when he nosed-dived into a
chocolate éclair.

Seated across from me in the restaurant booth, Evans rests
his hand on the edge of the table. With his thumb to the
outside and his smallest finger closest to his body, he looks as
if he's swung his left arm around his back and placed it to
the right of his body like a contortionist. But his reattached
hand, though miraculous, isn't as dexterous as it may sound.
He has limited range of motion with his fingers and wrist,
and in a resting position his digits are actually cupped upward as if he were holding open the paper wrapping of a cup-
cake. To keep his hand as active and as loose as possible,
Evans says he stands against the wall and rubs his fingers
across it, splaying them out to force the straightening motion doctors say is critical for continued growth of nerve tissue and acceptance of the transferred hand.

Continued acceptance is everything. Evans had been told
about another double amputee who ultimately had to lose
the transferred hand because it was rejected by his body. As a
result, the man needed a prosthetic and, with no other arm
to take it on and off, he required full-time care. If Evans's new
left-on-right arrangement didn't take, he would have followed a similar path. Although aware of the role of luck in
such matters, Evans also knew that the more diligent he was,

the better his chance of keeping the hand and the independence that would go with it. "People say I was so disciplined with therapy. Baloney. I was frustrated because I couldn't do anything." He was also eager to move out of the nursing home he'd been placed in for the eight months following the accident. "When the holidays came, the old people would just sit by the windows and cry."

Growing up in Decatur, Evans had a neighbor who was a policeman. He was a friendly man, recalls Evans, but then he lost a leg and went from gentle to mean. "He was feeling so sorry for himself and was just so bitter. I was afraid of turning into someone like him." Although he was once a baker, Evans never once discusses the things he can no longer do, and "bitter" strikes me as the last word that could ever apply to him.

Evans wanted out of that nursing home, and so he worked his hand, constantly. While building flexibility in his fingers, he remembers how one digit had a habit of staying upright after a lot of straightening exercises. Convenient maybe for a Yankees fan or a Massachusetts driver, less so for a happy, church-going guy from central Illinois. "It looked like I was flipping everyone off!"

Everything else was about finding ways to adapt. To put on his elastic-band watch, for example, he uses the ingenious method of holding a lamp harp (the wire part that goes around the bulb) upside-down between his legs. With his fingers, he puts the watch around the harp and pushes it down to begin expanding the strap. Then he puts his whole hand through so that his wrist, not the metal harp, takes over the job of expanding the watchband. When he removes his arm, the watch stays wrapped around his wrist. His technique for putting socks on with a coat hanger is even more ingenious and impossible to describe.

About a year after the accident, he spilled hot water while making coffee. Angry at first, Evans's usual grin quickly returned when he realized that he could feel the heat for the first time. The nerves were taking to their new setup and starting to regenerate. "I still can't tell how they got it hooked on at all," he says, holding his arm in the air. "I look at it and think of the vessels and stuff; it's like doing electrical wiring but in a tornado, with all those open nerves and everything all over the place. When I look at it now, I think: 'You're weird!' But then I'm glad the doctor made the decision he did because without it, I'd have to have a prosthetic. Putting one of those on is difficult, and I'd have to live in a nursing home."

On the matter of handedness, Evans's surgeon told *Left-hander* magazine—yes, there once was such a thing—that "the nerves that are controlling the left hand are actually coming from the right hand [nerve center]. So in a brain sense, I'd say that he's right-handed. But whether he is actually left-handed or right-handed is a good question. The brain has the plasticity to adapt to different things," he continued, as is clear by Evans's expanding in dexterity.

When I called Stephen Christman in Toledo to hear his take on Evans's handedness, he too would describe Evans as right-handed. Although the concept of a Southpaw is often associated with images of a baseball mitt or perhaps a left hand holding a pen, handedness is a neurological phenomenon. "Imagine," says Christman, "if some forensic investigators found a box filled with 100 human hands. There would be no way to reliably determine for each hand whether it belonged to a right- or left-handed person, with the exception perhaps of major calluses or something. But in terms of biology, there would be nothing because handedness is in the brain."

The control center for Evans's existing hand is situated where it has always been, in the left hemisphere. "I would think," adds Christman, "that his brain doesn't 'care' much what kind of hand is attached at the end of the right arm. It's as if this part of the brain were saying: 'I'm the left hemisphere and I've been controlling that hand all my life, and now something's weird down there where the nerves of the arm run into the nerves of the hand, but it's still sort of working, so that's fine.'"

And yet there's this: because the nerve endings of Evans's left arm were totally yanked out, he doesn't suffer from excruciating phantom pain, as is the case for many amputees. "Phantom pain usually occurs if the limb was painful before it was lost or amputated," explains Christman. But if someone touches Evans's left shoulder socket, where there were once nerves traveling down his arm and into his left hand, the only place where a nervous system response is manifest is the wrist and hand now on his *right* side. The first time this happened, Evans kept looking down at his hand, where he felt the contact, even though someone was touching his opposite shoulder. "So it shows up all the way over here," he says, lifting his right arm while looking down at his empty left side.

I have a hard time comprehending this, I confess, because there's no literal connection between the nerves in his shoulder and the nerves in his hand. Christman too is puzzled, but: "It's not uncommon for phantom sensations to project onto new areas of the body." One famous example is that of an amputee who, when touched on the face with a cotton swab, felt stimuli both on the face and in the phantom limb.[3] But that's because the regions responsible for control and sensation of hand and face are in adjacent spots in the brain. In that particular case, the part of the brain that used to control the arm was taken over or commandeered by the system for facial stimuli. For Evans, the nerves sending and receiving information to and from the hands are literally hemispheres apart. Nervous signals "would have to go from the touch of the left shoulder to the right hemisphere, to the left hemisphere, then down to the right arm to the transplanted left hand," says Christman. Chuckling, Evans says he doesn't get the mechanics of it either. But he assures me the sensation is real.

Evans thinks of himself as a natural right-hander because he was right-handed before the accident, but he says he's happy to be an honorary Southpaw: "I'm just glad I got a paw!" Nowadays, he says, between elastic and Velcro, he's got it made. Because he can squeeze his fingers together relatively tightly, he uses them as vice-like grips, enabling him to pick up his mail, unlock his front door, and even write. To write, Evans puts one knee down on the carpet. He then sets up the paper, usually with some weight on it because he has no backup hand to hold it still. He picks up a pen, holds it in his teeth, uncaps it with his hand, then delivers it to the nook between his third and fourth fingers, perpendicular to his palm. Squeezed this way, Evans's pen is upright and ready to write. "I've got nicer handwriting than the chicken scratch of most doctors," he says, leaning and squinting in laughter. Before I'd arrived in Decatur, Evans had taken the time to carefully write out—without my asking for it—a list of all his press coverage, with the news outlet name and year the article or television segment appeared. His writing has the squiggles of an elderly person's trembling penmanship but is entirely legible and has the balance and care of someone with a clear sense of tidiness. At Pastabilities, the Chumbawamba song "Tub Thumping" comes on the overhead radio—*I get knocked down, I get up again!*—triggering a memory of my weekend at Handwriting University, and for a moment I wonder what graphology experts would come up with to interpret Evans's personality through his shaky handwriting.

We finish our lunches and order tiramisu on Evans's recommendation. Over and over he says how lucky he is: that the train tore off his arm instead of carrying his whole body away, which surely would have killed him; for having the nerve endings pulled out so completely that he doesn't have phantom pain; to live in a place where everyone is so friendly and the waitresses know you by name and cut your food for you; and for the miraculous work of the doctors, who not only salvaged his limb but his quality of life as well.

Few people I've met on this journey are as instantly likeable as Evans. I tell him so and add that if I had the authority, I'd seat him at the roundtable of Southpaw elite right up there next to da Vinci and Babe Ruth. But he's far too humble for anything like that. "I'd just be the water boy," he says, laughing and leaning again. "Hook a water bottle onto my thumb, and I'm all set."

As for handedness and the meaning of life? "Whether you're right- or left-handed, it doesn't matter. How you deal with things is what makes a difference." After a bit of reflection, though, he adds that his experience has taught him that left-handed people are different because they "have to think things out just a bit more."

He's right. Evans, a master of adaptation, is referring to the fact that lefties have to spend nanoseconds here and there, every day, stepping back and reconfiguring how to operate in the world—the can opener, corkscrew, circular saw, fountain pen, and yes, even the classroom desk chair. It may not be, and usually isn't, a conscious process, but it happens, and it's a lifetime of additional movement calculus that right-handers' brains don't have to contend with. One Harvard psychologist, who happens to be my father, put it this way: "Lefties can never accept the world as it is presented to them, always reconfiguring spatial arrangements, implements, and the like from right-oriented to left-oriented. My guess? The same thing happens conceptually, and lefties are often re-imaging ideas and concepts because of their proclivity not to take things at face value."

How that slight but perpetual tweaking of perspective influences the lives and minds of left-handers, I'm not yet sure. But thanks to Evans, I leave Decatur reinvigorated, convinced that a plausible definition of Southpaw uniqueness is out there. And that I can find it.

CHAPTER 14

Sexy Beast

For there is often a struggle, and sometimes,
even more interestingly, a collusion between
the powers of pathology and creation.[1]

—*Oliver Sacks*, The Man Who Mistook His Wife for a Hat

"So, you wanna get zapped?"

"Um, will it hurt?" I ask.

"No, no. It won't hurt," says Tim Verstynen, a PhD student in psychology at Berkeley's Helen Wills Neuroscience Institute. Verstynen sounds sincere enough, but the guy also works in a windowless basement laboratory, sports a tattoo on his right arm, and has a slightly devilish laugh. He holds the blue paddle of the Magstim-brand transcranial magnetic stimulation machine as if it were a wooden racket for that ball-whacking beach game. With this paddle, however, the handler can induce electrical stimulus in the motor cortex of someone's brain, causing contraction of specific muscles in the extremities.

I shrug, poorly feigning casualness, and agree to get zapped. Verstynen tells me to sit with my left hand on my thigh, palm up, thumb and index finger in the shape of an "OK" sign. Holding the paddle to an area on the right side of my head, perhaps three inches north of my ear, he asks if I'm ready. I say yes, although I'm wondering whether we should start with my right hand in case things go awry. I'd hate to injure my left hand after all this.

Whack! I feel a sudden impact on my skull, more surprise than pain, like someone just flicked me. Because I'm nervous, I fail to watch my hand, which apparently moved. Verstynen zaps me a couple more times. Pinpointing the location in the brain corresponding to the muscles of the hand is actually pretty easy. Hands have a large area of representation in the cortex, probably because they're such important and intricate tools. I keep my eyes on my hand this time and sure enough, it twitches.

Through his research, Verstynen is busting myths about handedness and hemispheres, specifically the exclusivity of contralateral or cross-wired control. In one recent study, he investigated the workings of the brain during simple versus complex motor tasks. In so doing, he bumped into an unexpected difference between left- and right-handers. The goal was to determine whether it was the hands themselves or the brain's effect on hand function that accounts for variation in performance. In other words, when slicing onions, performance discrepancy between the left and right hands is obvious in the differing efficiency of movement of the hands and quality of the slices. But what's the root cause of that difference? Is it something qualitative about the hands themselves, or does it have to do with the brain? And is that difference detectable no matter the task?

Using brain-imaging technology known as functional magnetic resonance imaging, or fMRI, Verstynen asked right-handed subjects to move their fingers in a simple up-down motion, seeing how quickly the people could do so in a set block of time. As expected, the righties were more proficient (faster) at this task with the right hand than with the left. And as predicted, the actions resulted in firing or lighting up of activity on the left side of the brain.

Next he asked them to perform more complex, sequential movements, tapping their fingers against the thumb in a certain order, like a flutist silently reviewing a tune. Again, the righties were better with the dominant hand. But the fMRI also detected activation in the left hemisphere, even when righties were tapping away with their left hands. In simplest terms, something about this task requires the brain to recruit assistance from the left hemisphere. The motor control from the relevant side of the brain, in this case the right one, can't handle the task alone, probably because the left hemisphere specializes in tasks like ordering words in a sentence. The result was the same when performing a different style of complex task ("complex" compared to the simple, up-down motions), this time pressing fingers down in combinations resembling piano chords.

Lefties, however, defied prediction. With the simple task, the dominant hand was more proficient and, as expected, activation was visible in the right hemisphere. For the complex tasks, both hemispheres lit up, again, just like righties. But the lefties performed the complex tasks better with the right hand than they did with the left.

Initially, I was almost insulted by this data, as if the capability or very coordination of left-handers was at stake. But because so much of handedness and what we do with the hands is a function of how the brain works, taking offense to this stuff means completely missing the point. The research is a window into hemispheric differences. It also shows that Southpaws aren't a mirror image of right-handers.

Verstynen's work harkens back to wider questions of hemispheric specialization, evolution, and left-hemispheric responsibility for functions like language. To perform the planning and arranging task of tapping through different chords, the brain needs to access the control center or centers specialized for that kind of computation. For a simpler, speed-related task of just moving a finger up and down, the part of the brain controlling motor function can deal on its own. The reason left-handers were more adept at performing certain tasks with their right hands is probably because the right hand is hotwired to the left side of the brain, the side that choreographs those kinds of complex tasks, and not because of any dominant-hand deficiency.

One refreshing aspect of this study is that left-handers were critical in the effort to tease out useful results. More often than not, lefties are excluded from neurology research. "Almost always people just use right-handers as they're worried that mixing may add noise to the data," says John Duncan of the Medical Research Council's Cognition and Brain Sciences Unit in Cambridge, England. "As you're averaging brain activation data from different subjects, the fear is that the average could be spoiled by differences in laterality of activation. Of course, this could all be looked at properly with a large sample of subjects—but typically that's too expensive, so it isn't done."[2]

Righties are not all that interesting, adds Berkeley's Richard Ivry, because their behavior more closely follows a predicted outcome. With a righty moving his or her arm any which way, of course the left hemisphere will light up, but determining how much of that activation is motor function compared to cognitive function is difficult because both are housed in the left hemisphere. "Lefties are cool because they allow you to un-confound two hypotheses," says Ivry, untangling motor versus cognitive effects. Southpaws aid research in this way not simply because their hand preference differs but because left-handers' brains are literally wired differently.

The question that's been nagging for attention ever since Broca is *how* the brains of left-handed people differ or might differ, and what that means as far as how left-handers as people might differ. By this point I hope it's clear that lefties are not "in their right minds." But what *can* reasonably be said about the Southpaw brain without sounding like a snake-oil salesman? Something, after all, has to differentiate the brains of lefties from the brains of righties because differences in hand performance do not result from differences in the hands themselves. Because handedness is rooted in the brain, could other aspects of left-handers' brains differ as well?

Keep in mind that all left-handers do not necessarily have similarly organized minds. All brains vary. Not just in the sense that people and personalities are unique, but neurologically, the location and sometimes the size of control centers within the hemispheres vary as well. On the scale of populations, we know not all brains are the same for myriad reasons, such as the small percentage of individuals who have language lateralized to the right; a different minority who have such functions as language or spatial perception spread more evenly between the two hemispheres; and people with brain injuries who recover in unexpected ways, whose brains reconfigure themselves under new constraints.[3]

Language is a primary function used for studies about the nature of the brain, and research suggests that the proportion of people with language represented in both hemispheres is higher among Southpaws than among right-handers. The other way to look at this is that the less right-handed a person is, the more likely he is to be in the minority that has speech in the right hemisphere.[4] Yet as is becoming customary in this account, a quick reality check is required. Psychologists have also documented, for instance, that women process language more evenly between hemispheres than men. Different trends in brain activity for various subgroups of the human population have been and are constantly under investigation, which means ample caution is required when honing in on any one group or phenomenon. As Stanford University professor of biology and neurology Robert Sapolsky writes: "We still know squat about how the brain works."[5]

Yet certain neurological variations between lefties and righties have been documented. Asymmetry in the size of a brain structure known as the temporal plane is not found as reliably in left-handers, though any consequence of this variation has yet to be pinpointed.[6] What that says is that the *aggregate* for the two groups shows different levels of asymmetry, with a little more evenness detectable among the lefty group.

Scientists determine variation in brain organization a number of ways. One method is clinical cases, documenting how left- and right-handed stroke victims recover at different rates or with variable patterns of recovery of function. Likewise, people with injuries show differences in their regained functions, and those differences have been shown to sometimes correlate with handedness.[7] Another tool used to tease apart asymmetries in the brain is transcranial Doppler sonography, a technique that measures levels of brain activity on each side while a person is speaking.

But perhaps the biggest windfall in understanding brain organization, and subsequently how the brains of left-handers might differ from those of right-handers, is MRI and its younger cousin, fMRI. Try to picture a giant, cylindrical donut, a person lying inside, and harmless magnetic waves traveling through the brain, painting a real-time picture of the activity therein while the person responds to different questions or performs simple memory tasks.

A few years ago, a team of University of California at Los Angeles researchers examined fMRI brain scans of identical and fraternal twins, some left-handed and some right-handed. The study was led by neurologist Daniel Geschwind, a cousin of the Harvard researcher Norman Geschwind who theorized that high testosterone levels in the womb cause left-handedness. The UCLA Geschwind found, as one might expect, the most similarity in brain wiring among identical twins who're both right-handed. But identical twins with discordant handedness (one lefty, one righty) showed less similar brains. If it seems odd that identical twins could have discordant handedness despite having 100 percent identical genes, recall from Chapter 4 the idea of a chance gene for handedness applying to each individual, even twins.

This finding, although only one among scores indicating that brain structure is influenced by genetics, shows that differences in brain organization between lefties and righties are also highly influenced by genes. "Close to 99 percent of right-handers have language localized to the left hemispheres of the brain," says Geschwind. "But previous studies have shown that left-handed people don't mirror this model. We wanted to determine whether genetics explained this difference."[8] Indeed it did.

That the brains of left-handers do not precisely mirror those of right-handers crops up a lot in the scientific literature and is clear from studies such as the one conducted by the brain-zapping Verstynen. The consensus among experts is that at the population level, lefty brains are less lateralized—in other words more symmetrical. As a Southpaw, I'm curious what less asymmetry might mean in terms of the inner workings of my own brain, although once again this is a population-wide inference, and I may very well have a brain map that looks just like that of the righty who lives next door. Unfortunately, and frustratingly, the less lopsided nature of left-handers' brains is precisely why Southpaws are often excluded from most scientific research. Because we could muck up data about the specific function being analyzed, it's easier just to leave us out.

There are hints, however, that studying Southpaw brains may yield tantalizing results. British scientists recently reported, for instance, that left-handers' brains process visual information differently than those of right-handers. They used the same type of device Verstynen used on me to disrupt operations in one hemisphere or the other when subjects focused on wider-scope images, such as a forest, versus more detailed images, such as individual trees. If concentration was broken when the zapper was applied to one side, the scientists knew that that hemisphere was recruited for that type of visual processing; if concentration was unimpaired, that hemisphere wasn't participating in that function. They found that when right-handers concentrated on a macro-view, the right side of their brain was active, and for micro-views, the left. But for left-handers, the opposite was true.[9]

A few years ago neurologist Albert Galaburda told *The New York Times* that for brains of increased symmetry, "we do find more connections between the two hemispheres."[10] But what could more interhemispheric communication mean for Southpaws, or more precisely, the subset of people—some Southpaws and some righties—who actually have it? As discussed earlier, Stephen Christman's idea is that greater cross-hemispheric interaction may predispose some people to certain two-handed skills such as playing the violin, aptitude for music notwithstanding. Chris Niebauer has tried to extend this theory about interhemispheric communication to all sorts of inferences about belief systems and how we shape, hold, and change the beliefs that make us who we are.

What likely isn't going to emerge is a significant cognitive or intellectual superiority or inferiority for any particular group. When theories of left-handedness caused by birth stress or some kind of brain trauma reached their peak of popularity, researchers wanted to know whether this supposed pathological condition might also negatively impact higher mental functions.[11] Higher representation of left-handers among populations like schizophrenics, stutterers, and people with reading disabilities probably fed this curiosity. As neurologists Sally Springer and Georg Deutsch explain: "The same damage that produces the impairment also might be responsible for the shift to left-hand usage. It does not follow, however, that a similar relationship holds for unselected groups of subjects obtained outside of the clinical setting."[12] One review summarizing 14 studies about possible deficits for left-handers reported no difference between right- and left-handers in reading ability, with the exception of one examination suggesting left-handers scored slightly higher in achievement.[13]

The idea of Southpaw intellectual prowess hasn't found much empirical support either. For example, the popular belief that left-handers are disproportionately represented in the Mensa high-IQ society is based on flimsy data and has not been substantiated by any subsequent studies.[14] Another investigation in the United Kingdom involving more than 11,000 children found that "the effect [in intelligence difference] was so tiny as to be of interest only to statisticians."[15] Today, left-handedness resulting from some form of damage is a theory struggling for support and is further weakened by the dearth of data on meaningful cognitive impairment.

Then there's creativity. More than any other popular characterization of lefties is the notion that we possess a sort of artistic sixth sense. Even people who suspect that this isn't correct permit the idea to linger in the back of their minds, if for no other reason than the sheer romance of it. Until recently, I was pretty much the opposite. I'd humor a concept of lefty superiority for kicks when bonding with fellow Southpaws, yet I was aware that evidence of lefty creative prowess just wasn't there. I'd also read enough infuriated accounts from scholars about the gross exaggeration of hemispheric differences and the fiction of the creative right brain that I came to the deflating but scientifically honest conclusion that we're not more creative. Case closed, or so I thought.[16]

Michigan State University's Lauren Harris is one of many experts who has blasted the pseudoscience myth of the creative right brain. When I asked him point blank if lefties are more creative, I expected, and was sort of trying to induce, a tongue lashing. But this was his reasoned response: "I want to say, 'Which lefty?' It's certainly possible that one of the subgroups of left-handers does have certain different cognitive skills or patterns of skills from right-handers. There's some evidence, both anecdotal and documented, that left-handers are overrepresented in student artists, for example. There've been a dozen or more attempts to look for measures of creativity, but my guess is that it's a bit of a wash. The problem is, what do you mean by creative? But, I do think it's in the realm of possibility. . . . "

If watchdogs of careful research and antisensationalism are willing to entertain the possibility that certain lefties are more creative, what's my hang-up? Maybe I'm just not one of those creative Southpaws, able to think outside the proverbial box. Gradually, though, fragmented evidence has been accumulating all around me, indicating that a belief-updating event of my own may be in the forecast.

Discussing her Right Shift Theory, Marian Annett told me the persistence of left-handers within the human population would suggest an advantage to not carrying the right shift gene. "The main candidate for such an advantage, I think, is that among left-handed or mixed-handed people, you've got a chance for greater creativity. . . . There are strong trends in the data. A lot of evidence suggests that the percentage of non-right-handers is higher among those who're great mathematicians, for example. Not everyone, but over populations this would be an advantage." Annett also points to a slightly higher proportion of Southpaws in such sports as cricket, baseball, and tennis, but this argument sounds flimsy, especially in light of other, external factors that might attract and/or encourage Southpaws pursuing careers as professional athletes.

In 1995, the *American Journal of Psychology* reported that lefties scored higher on tests relating to divergent thinking and problem-solving.[17] An earlier study found that lefties are disproportionately represented among architects, and in 2004 researchers writing in *Neuropsychology* reported that for mathematically gifted teenagers, the two sides of the brain work together better.[18] Another paper reports that Pythagoras was left-handed, which isn't statistically relevant, but the same author also claims that left-handers are more represented among mathematicians than among a random population sample.[19] Discussing left-handers in politics, Harvard professor of cognition and education Howard Gardner was quoted saying that people with more symmetrical brains might have an edge with conceptualizing and planning: "It is probably not an accident that military leaders, who need to envision wide terrains, historically went into politics." Norman Schwarzkopf, Winston Churchill, George Patton, Colin Powell, Napoleon, Alexander the Great, and of course Andrew Kerr—lefties all of 'em.[20]

Finally, there's the somewhat fringe idea about handedness and "magical ideation," a term describing one's proclivity for believing in matters beyond the verifiable, be they supernatural forces, extrasensory perception, heaven's pearly gates, reincarnation, or palmistry. Wasn't it Diabolos Rex who mentioned that left-handers are more typically into occults?

New Zealander Michael Corballis describes a potential link between more brain symmetry, which left-handers have been shown to possess, and magical ideation. "Hemispheric asymmetry itself may lead to more decisive and controlled action, and perhaps a better ability to organize hierarchical processes, as in language, manufacture, and theory of mind. Those individuals who lack cerebral asymmetry [a.k.a. increased symmetry] may be more susceptible to superstition and magical thinking, but more creative and perhaps more spatially aware."[21]

One study found that the more mixed-handed the person, the higher the score on a magical ideation scale. To be perfectly clear, this doesn't mean lefties are clairvoyant. Rather, some studies suggest that Southpaws tend to believe in the possibility of such things more frequently. On the other hand, anecdotal evidence that lefties are highly represented in low-bullshit-tolerating professions such as journalism and science doesn't exactly support this notion.

As a prototypical strong left-hander myself, I tend not to believe in much outside the verifiable universe, which contradicts the theory—at first. My profile, however, gels with the magical ideation hypothesis when it's recalibrated as a degree-not-direction descriptor, with strong-handers like me, who have more asymmetrical brains, being less likely to possess this psychological trait.

In the late 1980s, other researchers linked magical ideation with "paranormal thought, delusional thought, and creativity, and suggested that these characteristics relate to heightened right-hemispheric activation."[22] This finding may also connect to more symmetrical brains and mixed-handedness, as hinted at by a 2004 study looking at mathematically gifted children whose brains, for certain cognitive tasks, demonstrated noticeably more symmetry than the brains of average-ability teenagers and children.[23]

The magical ideation line of thinking loops back to creativity when we consider findings indicating an increased proportion of left-handers who suffer from such disorders as schizophrenia. With due acknowledgment once again to Corballis for synthesis of this idea, it's plausible that schizophrenia and magical ideation sprout from similar neurological roots. Research demonstrating connections between mixed-handedness and either of these two conditions advances that plausibility.

Consider for a moment that there's a thin, perhaps blurred line between genius and mental illness. What if some types of genius stem from the same aspect of the brain—or influence on the brain—as, say, magical ideation and schizophrenia, and that subtle variation in the arrangement of certain brain circuits determines the difference between the next da Vinci, the next graphology believer, the next Hendrix-like guitar god, or the next schizophrenic?

Albert Einstein is a provocative example, if not a little confusing at first because his handedness is unclear. Laterality scholars have concluded that he was mixed-handed, although many popular articles and lists of famous lefties mistakenly label him as a Southpaw.[24] Examination of his brain after death showed unusual anatomical symmetry that, as Galaburda stated, can mean above-normal interhemispheric connections.[25] Then there's the fact that Einstein's genius is often linked with an imagination supercharged with imagery, a highly right hemisphere–dependent function. It was that kind of imagination that ignited questions leading eventually to the Theory of Relativity: what does a person on a moving train see compared with what a person standing still sees, and how would the body age if traveling near the speed of light in a spaceship compared to the aging process observed on Earth?

Is it such a stretch to speculate that Einstein landed on the fortunate end of the same brain organization spectrum upon which other, less lucky individuals land in the mental illness category? And what if handedness too is influenced by this organizational crapshoot? Another way to look at the possible link between creativity, magical ideation, and handedness is to ask whether Einstein's noggin was put together with just the right amount of unusual organization to bless him with extraordinary genius, whereas others, like schizophrenics, autistics, stutterers, or dyslexics are less fortunate (though one could argue that it is the genius who is less fortunate).

If all this business of brain organization rings familiar, that's because it fits nicely with what McManus proposes with his theory that handedness results from a gene coding for more variable brain organization. Einstein could have inherited this gene and its chance influence conferred unprecedented cerebral capabilities, whereas the chance component determining his handedness happened to land in the mixed-handed area of the continuum.

But maybe the gene in question codes for strong- versus mixed-handedness. That's what Christman would believe.

This gene would have conferred upon Einstein a more symmetrical brain and thus, possibly, exceptional interhemispheric communication. The benefits of that bolstered communication remain theoretical, but consider Kim Peek, the autistic "megasavant" who inspired the movie *Rain Man*. Peek has absolute recall of more than 9,000 books and an almost frightening knowledge of mathematics, music, and historical dates. Peek also has no corpus callosum; his brain is essentially a unified organ with such mysterious computing power that NASA researchers have begun investigating how it works.[26]

Elevated levels of left-brain/right-brain communication; high magical ideation scores; increased access to the belief-updater side of the brain; increased variability of brain organization; a potential subgroup with different "patterns of skills;" left-handers defying prediction—could all these concepts be circling similar coordinates of a real-world truth, not flushed out enough for a pinpoint landing, yet not so outlandish as to be discredited with eye-rolling incredulity?

If future research were to somehow verify that a propensity for magical ideation is what historically sets left-handers apart, the final question is what advantage, collectively, this trait offers our species? As discussed earlier, one reason for the relatively stable proportion of lefties in the human population may be diversity itself, whether in brain organization, as McManus's theory would suggest, or some other kind of genetic fitness that Bill Hopkins is still trying to deduce by examining chimpanzees. In the big picture, high scores in magical ideation probably provide little or no practical advantage in modern life, for the same reason that detectable discrepancies in cognitive ability between Southpaws and righties are of little or no practical importance; the differences are tiny, and people and cultures too complex for a single factor like this one to shape strongly who we are and how we think.[27]

Yet regarding evolution and the continued existence of left-handers, Corballis suggests one final, enchanting possibility for the benefit of magical ideation that "has to do with sexual selection rather than natural selection. Magical ideation may simply be sexy, as the peacock's tail to the peahen."[28] Like it or not, faith in things beyond earthly verification, whether in a church or on an astrological chart, is and probably always has been a core component of human civilization. Maybe religious or ideation-flavored spirituality bolsters one's likelihood for acceptance and possibly attraction as well. Prejudice against left-handers indicates that left-handedness alone may not have been such a desirable trait. But if left-handedness and the psychological characteristic of magical ideation are indeed cousins, then maybe left-handedness is, well, sexy.

Might I be biased toward this suggestion that people like me are extra-attractive? Come on: how could I not be? But what's wonderful about vague and ultimately unverifiable areas of human behavior such as creativity and magical ideation is that no one could ever really, absolutely, say this stuff is bogus. Besides, there's an elegance, if not a delightful absurdity, to this cyclical idea: some people may be inclined to believe in a sort of lofty, lefty otherness because as lefties or mixed-handers they are predisposed to believe in precisely that kind of thing. And so the reverse may also be

true: those who don't have faith in bolstered lefty special-
ness stemming from different brain wiring aren't, neurologically speaking, capable of having that faith anyway. Don't
be hard on them, though, for they can't be expected to
understand.

CHAPTER 15

Pilgrimage

Light is the left hand of darkness
and darkness the right hand of light.
Two are one, life and death . . . [1]

—*Ursula K. Le Guin*, The Left Hand of Darkness

W hen I was in college, I spent a semester studying abroad
in Western Samoa. One Sunday, I decided to attend a
service at the giant egg-shaped Bahá'í temple. I remember
wondering why the followers of this supposed world faith
would locate one of their seven Houses of Worship in the
middle of a mountainous, impossibly remote Pacific island.
Other temples are in Chicago, Sydney, Delhi, Frankfurt—
populous world cities the lot of them. But the outskirts of
Apia, Western Samoa?

I don't know much about the Bahá'í faith, and I've forgotten most of what I learned about Samoa with the exception of the words *faguvai* and *matatioata*, which mean
water-bottle and sunglasses, respectively. But during the past
year of Southpaw searching, I've learned that places don't
possess meaning so much as we assign it to them. Even if the

rationale to locate a Bahá'í temple in Samoa was nothing more than a shrug, once it was built and somebody felt it was special, from that moment on the place carried indisputable significance because people, somewhere, had infused it with meaning through belief.

When I heard about Left Hand, West Virginia, a few years ago, I knew I had to visit, to see for myself whether the lefty vibe might somehow be intensified in such a place, and whether it might warrant a Southpaw version of a Bahá'í House of Worship. I called Charlie Smith, the Roane County clerk, to ask about the history of the town, but there was precious little to learn. "I think it's named after a fork in a river or something like that," said White. "But there's really not much there, just a sign and a post office." White did mention an elderly gentleman in nearby Spencer, an amateur historian who might be able to help me. Unfortunately, in the months between that first call and my mid-October arrival in town, the history buff had died.

———◆———

"You want to know about Left Hand? Well, how fast can you blink?" This is the common refrain when I ask people in nearby Spencer what they can tell me about life in Left Hand. I'm also told that the hamlet is exactly 22 miles south. I set the odometer so as not to miss it. The road whips past chiseled streaks of rock flanking hillsides, through the towns of Clover and Looneyville. Finally, I see the green sign, "Left Hand," above the word "unincorporated."

Morning shadows shroud much of the town, but higher up on the slopes the late autumn yellows and oranges glow in the sunlight. I spot the tiny post office, and then the school building. The few side roads are dotted with photogenic barns; not-so photogenic, dilapidated front porches with pumpkins and old air-conditioners; and front yards with satellite dishes and yet-to-be-stacked piles of chopped firewood. Although the pastures along Linden Tariff and Broad Run Roads are steeper and smaller than the fields of the Scottish Borderlands, the pastoral scene reminds me of Jedburgh and the legacy of Andrew Kerr.

A car idles in front of the Left Hand Independent Baptist Church, and I see a guy walking around to the back of the building. John Dye is turning on the gas so the church will be warm for services in an hour. Although not a native Left Hander, nor a left-hander, Dye "married a local girl" and has lived here for 31 years.

I ask him to recommend a hill I can walk up to gain a little perspective. Dye, staring down at me through large, square glasses, says there's not much to see in Left Hand. "Just a post office and a school," he says. But I'm determined to walk somewhere, and I ask about the semi-cleared path for the gas main just down the road. Dye shakes his head and says he doesn't want me getting all wet from the high grasses and shrubs still covered in dew. "And there's brambles too." He suggests instead an old logging road back down Linden Tariff Road. "That [rental car] won't get up it, but a four-wheel-drive vehicle could. If someone asks, just tell 'em you spoke with John Dye."

I find the road easily enough and park just off the street. The old uneven path ascends a west-facing slope into the woods, bringing me past a rusted-out oil pump, rotted stumps, and encroaching beech and maple saplings.

Then I almost step on it: a brain. Beneath a canopy of yellow beech leaves, staring up at me like some oversized fossil, is a rock about the size of a honeydew melon, eerily resembling a human brain. True, people often see what they want to see, but I *swear* this is the brainiest-looking rock you've ever seen, complete with a well-defined fracture down the middle, splitting it into two symmetrical hemispheres. Its color is a mixture of gray and brick hues. Underneath a few feet of soil and sediment, West Virginia is pretty much all rock, yet this one looks out of place on the mostly cleared road, and despite myself I contemplate whether some supernatural force planted it here for me to discover.

I kneel down for a closer look at what would roughly be the right motor cortex—the same area that a few weeks earlier Tim Verstynen had zapped in my own brain—and spot a nickel-sized patch of bright green lichen. It's like nothing else anywhere on the otherwise dark-colored rock. "There's nothing biological in the brain that tells us if a person is left-handed or right-handed," Chris McManus had said in his London office months before. That doesn't mean, however, that there's nothing there. "There must be *something* in the brain that makes left-handers, left-handers," Marian Annett had told me. My view? I too believe something's there, something subtle that someone like Nobutaka Hirokawa will eventually stumble upon.

Heading back through the woods of Left Hand, I got to thinking about all brains, not just those of left-handers. If this quest has led to any unifying theme, perhaps it's one of engineered uniqueness. Every personality is different, that much is a given. But I think we sometimes overlook the fact that every person's brain is literally wired differently, sometimes dramatically so. Culture, geography, religion, education, and race are all primary ingredients in the stew of human diversity. Yet perhaps the diversity in configuration and operation of the very organ that is the engine of our thoughts is the greatest of all determinants of human variability. Whether there's a right shift gene out there that makes most people right-handed, or whether there's a gene coding for an extra dash of scrambled brain organization, or whether some other left-handedness theory turns out to be the big winner—whatever its ultimate cause, the deceptively complicated matter of left-handedness serves as a reminder of the variability of brain organization, and by extension the diversity of thinking within our species.

During my trip to Paris to see Broca's brains, I thought about how the magic of a place can, in part, be deconstructed with the help of details. A run along the Seine; ornate architecture on the tiniest of side streets; fresh *pain au chocolat* four times in one day; the accordion store on Rue Daguerre. But like a photograph, an inventory of details can't encapsulate the essence of a place entirely because much of what makes a place special is the feeling we have when we're there. It's a real feeling to be sure, but often one beyond precise identification. Why do I love Paris? What does my friend Kataoka find so compelling about that hilltop shrine in Japan? Why does John Evans only feel at home in Decatur, Illinois, why do West Virginians believe there's magic in the hollows of Roane County, and what is it that makes your favorite spot your favorite spot? In the end, after all the description and carefully chosen adjectives, what makes a place special is that certain *je ne sais quoi*. It's real but difficult to pin down.

The same trick of eluding precise identification could also help with the question of what makes left-handers unique. Their difference is subtle enough to be outside the reach of an easily packaged notion like bolstered creativity, but noticeable enough to warrant the interest of still-perplexed researchers. Thankfully, scientists have steered us away from pseudoscience myths and fallacies derived from past research. At the same time, they've gathered substantial evidence that Southpaws are not the mirror image of right-handers, and that as a population left-handers have brains that are different—not starkly different, like the left and right hemispheres, but not trivial in their differences either. Scientists have even suggested that left-handedness has persisted through the ages because those individuals, more likely to believe in higher powers and other-worldly forces, are sexy, at least in the Darwinian sense. In the meantime, scholars continue to debate results from studies of brain asymmetry, interhemispheric communication, the handedness of apes, and the prospects of a gene conferring extra brain variation on one subgroup of the population.

The resolution of the lefty picture isn't yet sharp enough for definitive interpretation. All we can depend on, for now, is that real but only partially describable feeling. So the next time someone asks how left-handers are different, reply by saying they're special. And that science can prove it.

Acknowledgments

I t would be inaccurate to say that this book would not exist without the guidance, assistance, and sharp editing
skill of other people. It would be fair to say, however, that
without their help, this book would be a mess.

First, I'd like to thank the scientists—all of them, really,
whether they study handedness, climate change, or colon
cancer. They're the ones who are truly chasing the mysteries, trying to make sense of our world. I'd especially like to
thank those researchers who were so patient with me and
my demands on their time. Most were unquestionably sup-
portive, cognizant of the fact that layperson-level science
writing, despite simplification and the risk of misrepresenta-
tion, is worth it. Those who were particularly generous include: Michael Corballis, Chris McManus, Lauren Harris,
Bill Hopkins, Robert Sainburg, Stephen Christman, Marian Annett, Jane Healey, Tim Verstynen, Rich Ivry, Chris
Niebauer, Noah Helman, David Weld, Jason Dimmig, and
Nobutaka Hirokawa.

Outside of academia I had an equally gracious network of
people who helped me complete this project. Even though
I'm bound to miss a few, special thanks must go to: John

Evans, Diabolos Rex, and Rabbi Lawrence Kushner; Mie and Tsutomu Waki in Osaka, Paul P. de Saint-Maur at the Musée Dupuytren in Paris, and John Swan, Duncan Woods, and Jessie Fraser in Jedburgh; Sara Kotora at Juniata College; Stan Levin and Ed Levien in Bethesda, Maryland; Sara Worman at Anything Left-Handed in London; Sylvie Dugal, Ghanshyam Birla, and Francis Dejardins with the Vedic Palmistry Network; and John Dye and Leah and Ken Truman of Left Hand, West Virginia.

As for influential teachers and mentors, thank you Doug Fricke, Jack Kruse, Ron Powers, John Elder, Tamar Mayer, and especially Bill Woo. The same goes for my friends, in particular Joshua Davis, Heather Wax, and Coert Voorhees. When the three of you aren't editing my stuff with almost scary acumen, you're motivating me with your own successes. Joe Treen at *Discover* offered valuable input, for which I'm also grateful. Thank you to Giles Anderson, my agent, as well as everyone at Da Capo Press. You've made this process smooth and enjoyable.

To my siblings and parents, thank you for being a great family. If there is anything too much travel, psychology research, and encounters with the occasional odd duck can teach you, it's that coming home to family can be a real joy. Thank you especially Mom and Pop for the opportunities and unconditional support you've given to me in every endeavor.

Finally, thank you, Nicola. You are the most magnificent partner I could ever imagine. I love you.

Notes

Preface

1. As reported by BBC News, October 26, 2003.

Chapter One

1. Jerome S. Bruner, *On Knowing: Essays for the Left Hand* (New York: Atheneum, 1965), 8.

2. http://www.wordorigins.org/wordors.htm; http://www.word-detective.com/093098.html; other sites and citations as well.

Chapter Two

1. John Gay, as quoted in Stanley Coren, *The Left-Hander Syndrome: The Causes and Consequences of Left-Handedness* (New York: Vintage Books, 1992), 11.

2. Michael Corballis, *The Lopsided Ape: Evolution of the Generative Mind* (New York: Oxford University Press, 1991), 82.

3. Coren, 18.

4. Ibid.

5. Michael Henry Barsley, *The Other Hand: An Investigation into the Sinister History of Left-Handedness* (New York: Hawthorn Books, 1967).

6. Vladimir Nabokov, *Bend Sinister* (New York: Vintage Books, 1990; first published by McGraw-Hill, 1947), xii.

7. Chris McManus, *Right Hand Left Hand: The Origins of Asymmetry in Brains, Bodies, Atoms, and Cultures* (Cambridge, Mass.: Harvard University Press, 2002), 21–23.

8. William Lee Berdel Martin and Monique Barbosa Freitas, "Mean Mortality Among Brazilian Left- and Right-Handers: Modification or Selective Elimination." *Laterality* 7:1 (2002):31–44.

9. Geoffrey Nunberg, "Who's a Leftist Now? It Depends on Where You Stand," *International Herald Tribune* August 19, 2003.

10. Ibid.

Chapter Three

1. Richard Restak, *The New Brain: How the Modern Age Is Rewiring Your Brain* (New York: Rodale, 2003), 3.

2. S. Finger, *Origins of Neuroscience: A History of Explorations into Brain Function* (Oxford: Oxford University Press, 1994). (As cited in upcoming article in *Lancet Neurology*.)

3. Michael Corballis, *From Hand to Mouth: The Origins of Language* (Princeton, N.J.: Princeton University Press, 2002), 164.

4. Francis Schiller, *Paul Broca: Explorer of the Brain* (New York: Oxford University Press, 1992), 182.

5. Ibid., 184.

6. Ibid., 182.

7. Ibid., 180.

8. "Rigorously" is from Broca, as cited in Schiller, 187.

9. Chris McManus, personal interview, April 2004.

10. Oliver Sacks, *The Man Who Mistook His Wife for a Hat* (New York: Harper & Row, 1970), 3.

11. Carl Sagan, *Broca's Brain: Reflections of the Romance of Science* (New York: Presidio Press, 1974), 9–10.

12. Broca, as cited in Chris McManus, *Right Hand Left Hand: The Origins of Asymmetry in Brains, Bodies, Atoms, and Cultures* (Cambridge, Mass.: Harvard University Press, 2002), 13.

13. Acknowledgment is due to Lauren Harris of the University of Michigan for generous explanations on this subject.

14. McManus, 13.

15. Ibid., 195.

16. UCLA press release, March 4, 2002: "Left-Handed Persons' Brains Organized Differently Than Right-Handers, UCLA Scientists Discover."

17. Robert Ornstein, *The Right Mind: Making Sense of the Hemispheres* (San Diego: Harcourt Brace & Company, 1997), 83.

18. Lauren Harris, personal interview, December 2004.

Chapter Four

1. Stanley Coren, *The Left-Hander Syndrome: The Causes and Consequences of Left-Handedness* (New York: Vintage Books, 1992), 52; Sally P. Springer and Georg Deutsch, *Left Brain, Right Brain* (New York: W. H. Freeman, 1993), 128.

2. "A Possible Reason Why Left-Handedness Is Rare but Not Extinct," *The Economist*, December 9, 2004.

3. As cited in Coren, 13.

4. Chris McManus, *Right Hand Left Hand: The Origins of Asymmetry in Brains, Bodies, Atoms, and Cultures* (Cambridge, Mass.: Harvard University Press, 2002), 157.

5. Ibid., 294.

6. From an interview with Richard Ivry, September 2004.

7. As summarized by Michael L. Kruger in *Perceptual & Motor Skills* 98:1 (2004):44.

8. H. Kieler, S. Cnattingius, B. Haglund, J. Palmgren, and O. Axelsson, "Sinistrality a Side-Effect of Prenatal Sonography: A Comparative Study of Young Men," *Epidemiology* November 2001: 618–623.

9. Helle Kieler, email to the author, June 2005.

10. Walter McKeever, "An X-linked Three Allele Model of Hand Preference and Hand Posture for Writing," *Laterality* 9:2 (2004):175.

11. "Social Interaction Determines Left- or Right-Side Bias," *Biotech Week* March 24, 2004:680.

12. McManus, 148.

13. Ibid., 156, 206.

14. Michael Corballis, *From Hand to Mouth: The Origins of Language* (Princeton, N.J.: Princeton University Press, 2002), 170.

15. Marian Annett, *Handedness and Brain Asymmetry: The Right Shift Theory* (New York: Psychology Press, 2002), 315.

16. Jocelyn Selim, "Out of Left Field," *Discover* January 2002.

17. Matt Ridley, *Genome: The Autobiography of a Species in 23 Chapters* (New York: Perennial, 1999), 2.

18. Laura Spinney, "A Left-Brain/Right-Brain Conundrum Revisited," *TheScientist.com* 18:7 (2004).

19. Michael Corballis, unpublished paper received by author in 2004.

20. McManus, 160.

21. Ibid., 161.

22. Ibid., 35.

Chapter Five

1. Haruki Murakami, "Where I'm Likely to Find It," *New Yorker* May 2, 2005:93.

2. Nikolai Leskov, *The Enchanted Wanderer, Selected Tales*, translated by David Magarshack (New York: The Modern Library, 2003), 235.

3. Carl Sagan, *Broca's Brain: Reflections of the Romance of Science* (New York: Presidio Press, 1974), 66–67.

Chapter Six

1. Frank R. Wilson, *The Hand: How Its Use Shapes the Brain, Language, and Human Culture* (New York: Vintage Books, 1998), 33.

2. Michael Corballis, unpublished paper received by author in 2004.

3. Michael Corballis, *The Lopsided Ape: Evolution of the Generative Mind* (New York: Oxford University Press, 1991), 104.

4. Wilson, 58.

5. Steven Pinker, *The Best American Science and Nature Writing 2004* (New York: Houghton Mifflin, 2004), xxi.

6. Carl Sagan, *Broca's Brain: Reflections of the Romance of Science* (New York: Presidio Press, 1974), 10.

7. Laura Spinney, "A Left-Brain/Right-Brain Conundrum Revisited," *TheScientist.com* 18:7 (2004).

8. Corballis, unpublished paper, 5.

9. Chris McManus, *Right Hand Left Hand: The Origins of Asymmetry in Brains, Bodies, Atoms, and Cultures* (Cambridge, Mass.: Harvard University Press, 2002), 226.

10. Marian Annett, personal interview, January 2005.

11. Michael Corballis, *From Hand to Mouth: The Origins of Language* (Princeton, N.J.: Princeton University Press, 2002), 169.

12. Annett, personal interview, January 2005.

13. McManus, 229.

14. McManus, personal interview, April 2004.

15. Corballis, *From Hand to Mouth*, 172.

16. Corballis, unpublished paper.

17. Corballis, email to the author, February 2005.

18. Corballis, *From Hand to Mouth*, 172.

19. Klar, Amar J. S., "Human Handedness and Scalp Hair-Whorl Direction Develop from a Common Genetic Mechanism," *Genetics* 165 (September 2003):269–276.

20. McManus, personal interview, April 2004.

Chapter Seven

1. Nikolai Leskov, *The Enchanted Wanderer, Selected Tales*, translated by David Magarshack (New York: The Modern Library, 2003), 224.

2. Michael Corballis, *From Hand to Mouth: The Origins of Language* (Princeton, N.J.: Princeton University Press, 2002), 167.

3. Ibid., 168.

4. William Calvin, *A Brief History of the Mind: From Apes to Intellect and Beyond* (New York: Oxford University Press, 2004), 94.

5. Frank R. Wilson, *The Hand: How Its Use Shapes the Brain, Language, and Human Culture* (New York: Vintage Books, 1998), 27.

6. Calvin, 95.

7. Corballis, *Lopsided Ape: Evolution of the Generative Mind* (New York: Oxford University Press, 1991), 103.

8. Robert Sainburg, personal interview, October 2004.

9. Ibid.

10. Yves Guiard, as cited in Wilson, 159.

11. Sainburg, personal interview, October 2004.

12. Jocelyn Selim, "Out of Left Field," *Discover* January 2002.

13. Eric Scigliano, "Through the Eye of an Octopus," *Discover* October 2003.

14. Calvin, 159.

Chapter Eight

1. Marian Annett, personal interview, January 2005.

2. Sally P. Springer and Georg Deutsch, *Left Brain, Right Brain* (New York: W. H. Freeman, 1993), 139.

3. Chris McManus, *Right Hand Left Hand: The Origins of Asymmetry in Brains, Bodies, Atoms, and Cultures* (Cambridge, Mass.: Harvard University Press, 2002), 163–164.

4. Ibid.; Stanley Coren, *The Left-Hander Syndrome: The Causes and Consequences of Left-Handedness* (New York: Vintage Books, 1992).

Chapter Nine

1. John Donne, "To the Countess of Bedford," *Poems of John Donne*, Volume II (London: Lawrence & Bullen, 1896), 15–17.

2. Stephen Christman, personal interview, October 2004.

3. Chris McManus, *Right Hand Left Hand: The Origins of Asymmetry in Brains, Bodies, Atoms, and Cultures* (Cambridge, Mass.: Harvard University Press, 2002), 153.

4. John Illman, "Taking Sides," *New Scientist* July 14, 2001:36–37.

5. Steven Johnson, *Mind Wide Open: Your Brain and the Neuro-science of Everyday Life* (New York: Scribner, 2004), 6. Johnson credits Jim Robbins's *A Symphony in the Brain* as the source for the borrowed metaphor.

6. Robert Ornstein, *The Right Mind: Making Sense of the Hemispheres* (San Diego: Harcourt Brace & Company, 1997), 68.

7. *The Neurosurgeon's Interest in the Corpus Callosum*, http://www.its.caltech.edu/~jbogen/text/NeurosInterestCC.html.

8. Johnson, 29.

9. "Brainpower as Easy as X and Y," *CNN.com*, February 14, 2005. http://www.cnn.com/2005/TECH/science/02/14/gender.brain/index.html.

10. From Christman interview, citing Walter F. Daniel and Ronald A. Yeo, "Accident Proneness and Handedness," *Biological Psychiatry* (1994):499.

11. V. S. Ramachandran, *Phantoms in the Brain: Probing the Mysteries of the Human Mind* (New York: Quill, 1998), 141.

Chapter Ten

1. Karl Marx, *Karl Marx, Friedrich Engels, Collected Works, Vol. I: Karl Marx, 1835–1843* (London: Lawrence and Wishart, 1975), 622, as quoted in Chris McManus, *Right Hand Left Hand: The Origins of Asymmetry in Brains, Bodies, Atoms, and Cultures* (Cambridge, Mass.: Harvard University Press, 2002).

2. Michael Corballis points out that nearly 30 years ago he, and others, suggested "all biological asymmetries, including handedness and the asymmetry of the heart, could be related to a general development gradient favoring the left," and that Lewis Wolpert even implicated part of cilia as the responsible actor. See M. C. Corballis and M. J. Morgan, "On the Biological Basis of Human Laterality: Evidence for a Maturational Left-Right Gradient," *The Behavioral & Brain Sciences* 2 (1978):261–268. Also see Wolpert's article on page 325 of the same issue.

3. McManus, 84.

4. Juan Carlos Izpisua Belmonte, "How the Body Tells Left from Right," *Scientific American* June 1999:42–43.

5. McManus, 117.

6. Martina Brueckner, email to the author, February 2005.

7. Nobutaka Hirokawa, personal interview, September 21, 2004.

8. Howard Hughes Medical Institute press release, May 12, 2005: "Left- or Right-Brain? Genes May Tell the Story." http://www.hhmi.org/news/walsh2.html.

Chapter Eleven

1. Richard Ivry, personal communication, September 2004.

2. "Lefthandedness: Today Is Official Left-Handers' Day. Read Our Web Guide to the Other Side." *The Guardian* August 13, 2002.

Chapter Twelve

1. Michael Corballis, *The Lopsided Ape: Evolution of the Generative Mind* (New York: Oxford University Press, 1991), 86.

2. Jane M. Healey, *Loving Lefties: How to Raise Your Left-Handed Child in a Right-Handed World* (New York: Pocket Books, 2001), 108.

3. Stanley Coren, *The Left-Hander Syndrome: The Causes & Consequences of Left-Handedness* (New York: Vintage Books, 1992); Corballis.

4. Chris McManus, *Right Hand Left Hand: The Origins of Asymmetry in Brains, Bodies, Atoms, and Cultures* (Cambridge, Mass.: Harvard University Press, 2002), 148.

5. McManus, email to the author, August 2004.

6. Peter Hepper, email to the author, August 2004.

7. Laura Spinney, "Handedness Develops in the Womb," *New Scientist* July 22, 2004.

8. McManus, 165.

9. Ibid., 165–167.

10. "Seat with a View," *New Scientist* February 17, 2001.

11. McManus, 167.

12. Ibid., 156.

Chapter Thirteen

1. John Irving, *The Fourth Hand* (New York: Ballantine Books, 2001), 61.

2. Frank W. Wilson, *The Hand: How Its Use Shapes the Brain, Language, and Human Culture* (New York: Vintage Books, 1998), 258.

3. V. S. Ramachandran and Sandra Blakeslee, *Phantoms in the Brain: Probing the Mysteries of the Human Mind* (New York: Quill, 1998).

Chapter Fourteen

1. Oliver Sacks, *The Man Who Mistook His Wife for a Hat* (New York: Harper & Row, 1970), 18.

2. John Duncan, email to the author.

3. Robert Ornstein, *The Right Mind: Making Sense of the Hemispheres* (San Diego: Harcourt Brace, 1997), 83.

4. Michael Corballis, *From Hand to Mouth: The Origins of Language* (Princeton, N.J.: Princeton University Press, 2002), 171.

5. Robert Sapolsky, "Bugs in the Brain," *Scientific American* March 2003.

6. Lauren Harris, personal interview, winter 2004.

7. Jane M. Healey, personal interview, July 2004.

8. UCLA press release, March 4, 2002: "Left-Handed Persons' Brains Organized Differently than Right-Handers, UCLA Scientists Discover."

9. As reported by *BBC News*, February 7, 2005 (http://news.bbc .co.uk/1/hi/health/4242419.stm).

10. "Forget Left-Wing: Say Hello to Left-Handed Politics." *The New York Times* January 23, 2000.

11. Sally P. Springer and Georg Deutsch, *Left Brain, Right Brain* (New York: W. H. Freeman, 1993), 140.

12. Ibid., 140.

13. Ibid.

14. Chris McManus, *Right Hand Left Hand: The Origins of Asymmetry in Brains, Bodies, Atoms, and Cultures* (Cambridge, Mass.: Harvard University Press, 2002), 297.

15. Ibid., 297–298.

16. Corballis, 182.

17. "Forget Left-Wing."

18. Harnam Singh and Michael W. O'Boyle, "Interhemispheric Interaction During Global-Local Processing in Mathematically Gifted Adolescents, Average-Ability Youth, and College Students," *Neuropsychology* 18:2 (2004).

19. Catriona Byrne, "The Left-Handed Pythagoras," *Math Intelligencer* 12:3 (1990):52–53.

20. "Forget Left-Wing."

21. Corballis, 182.

22. Michael Corballis, unpublished paper received by author in 2004, 9.

23. Ibid.

24. McManus, 301.

25. Michael D Lemonick, "Was Einstein's Brain Built for Brilliance?" *Time* June 28, 1999.

26. Helena De Bertodano, "The Original Rain Man," *The Week* March 4, 2005.

27. Springer and Deutsch, 142.

28. Corballis, 180.

Chapter Fifteen

1. Ursula K. Le Guin, *The Left Hand of Darkness* (New York: Ace Books, 1969), 233–234.

Bibliography

Annett, Marian. *Handedness and Brain Asymmetry: The Right Shift Theory*. New York: Psychology Press, 2002.

Barsley, Michael Henry. *The Other Hand: An Investigation into the Sinister History of Left-Handedness*. New York: Hawthorn Books, 1967.

Berdel Martin, William Lee, and Monique Barbosa Freitas. "Mean Mortality among Brazilian Left- and Right-Handers: Modification or Selective Elimination." *Laterality* 7, no. 1 (2002).

Biotech Week, "Social Interaction Determines Left- or Right-Side Bias," 24 March 2004: 680.

Bogen, Joseph E. "The Neurosurgeon's Interest in the Corpus Callosum." In *A History of Neurosurgery*, ed. S. H. Greenblatt, T. F. Dagi, and M. H. Epstein. Park Ridge, IL: American Association of Neurological Surgeons, 1997. http://www.its.caltech.edu/~jbogen/text/NeurosInterestCC.html.

Byrne, Catriona. "The Left-Handed Pythagoras." *Math Intelligencer* 12, no. 3 (1990): 52–53.

Calvin, William. *A Brief History of the Mind: From Apes to Intellect and Beyond*. New York: Oxford University Press, 2004.

CNN.com, "Brainpower as Easy as X and Y," 14 February 2005. http://www.cnn.com/2005/TECH/science/02/14/gender.brain/index.html.

Corballis, M. C., and M. J. Morgan. "On the Biological Basis of Human Laterality: I. Evidence for a Maturational Left-Right Gradient." *The Behavioral & Brain Sciences* 2 (1978): 261–268.

Corballis, Michael. *From Hand to Mouth: The Origins of Language*. Princeton, NJ: Princeton University Press, 2002.

————. *The Lopsided Ape: Evolution of the Generative Mind.* New York: Oxford University Press, 1991.

Coren, Stanley. *The Left-Hander Syndrome: The Causes and Consequences of Left-Handedness.* New York: Vintage Books, 1992.

De Bertodano, Helena. "The Original Rain Man." *The Week,* 4 March 2005.

Economist, "A Possible Reason Why Left-Handedness Is Rare But Not Extinct," 9 December 2004.

Finger, S. *Origins of Neuroscience: A History of Explorations into Brain Function.* New York: Oxford University Press, 1994.

Gay, John, as quoted in Stanley Coren. *The Left-Hander Syndrome: The Causes and Consequences of Left-Handedness.* New York: Vintage Books, 1992.

Guiard, Yves, as cited in Frank Wilson. *The Hand: How Its Use Shapes the Brain, Language, and Human Culture.* New York: Vintage Books, 1998.

Healey, Jane M. *Loving Lefties: How to Raise Your Left-Handed Child in a Right-Handed World.* New York: Pocket Books, 2001.

Illman, John. "Taking Sides." *New Scientist,* 14 July 2001: 36–37.

Irving, John. *The Fourth Hand.* New York: Ballantine Books, 2001.

Izpisua Belmonte, Juan Carlos. "How the Body Tells Left from Right." *Scientific American,* June 1999: 42–43.

Johnson, Steven. *Mind Wide Open: Your Brain and the Neuroscience of Everyday Life.* New York: Scribner, 2004.

Klar, Amar J. S. "Human Handedness and Scalp Hair-Whorl Direction Develop from a Common Genetic Mechanism." *Genetics* 165 (September 2003): 269–276.

Kruger, Michael L. "Relation of Handedness with Season of Birth of Professional Baseball Players Revisited." *Perceptual & Motor Skills* 98, no.1 (2004): 44.

Le Guin, Ursula K. *The Left Hand of Darkness.* New York: Ace Books, 1969.

Lemonick, Michael D. "Was Einstein's Brain Built for Brilliance?" *Time,* 28 June 1999.

Leskov, Nikolai. *The Enchanted Wanderer: Selected Tales.* Translated by David Magarshack. New York: The Modern Library, 2003.

Marx, K. *Karl Marx, Frederick Engels, Collected Works, Vol. I: Karl Marx, 1835–1843*. London: Lawrence and Wishart, 1975.

McKeever, Walter. "An X-Linked Three Allele Model of Hand Preference and Hand Posture for Writing." *Laterality* 9, no. 2 (2004).

McManus, Chris. *Right Hand Left Hand: The Origins of Asymmetry in Brains, Bodies, Atoms, and Cultures*. Cambridge, MA: Harvard University Press, 2002.

Murakami, Haruki. "Where I'm Likely to Find It." *New Yorker*, 2 May 2005.

Nabokov, Vladimir. *Bend Sinister*. New York: McGraw Hill, 1947.

New Scientist, "Seat with a View," 17 February 2001.

New York Times, "Forget Left-Wing: Say Hello to Left-Handed Politics," 23 January 2000.

Numberg, Geoffrey. "Who's a Leftist Now? It Depends on Where You Stand." *International Herald Tribune*, 19 August 2003.

Oldfield, R. C. "The Assessment and Analysis of Handedness: The Edinburgh Inventory." *Neuropsychologia* 9 (1971): 97–113.

Ornstein, Robert. *The Right Mind: Making Sense of the Hemispheres*. San Diego, CA: Harcourt Brace, 1997.

Pinker, Steven. *The Best American Science and Nature Writing 2004*. New York: Houghton Mifflin, 2004.

Ramachandran, V. S., and Sandra Blakeslee. *Phantoms in the Brain: Probing the Mysteries of the Human Mind*. New York: Quill, 1998.

Restak, Richard. *The New Brain: How the Modern Age Is Rewiring Your Brain*. Rodale, 2003.

Ridley, Matt. *Genome: The Autobiography of a Species in 23 Chapters*. New York: Perennial, 1999.

Sacks, Oliver. *The Man Who Mistook His Wife for a Hat*. New York: Harper & Row, 1970.

Sagan, Carl. *Broca's Brain: Reflections of the Romance of Science*. New York: Presidio Press, 1974.

Sapolsky, Robert. "Bugs in the Brain." *Scientific American*, March 2003.

Schiller, Francis. *Paul Broca: Explorer of the Brain*. New York: Oxford University Press, 1992.

Scigliano, Eric. "Through the Eye of an Octopus." *Discover*, October 2003.

Selim, Jocelym. "Out of Left Field." *Discover,* January 2002.

Soldal, Hildegunn. "Lefthandedness." *The Guardian*, 13 August 2002.

Spinney, Laura. "A Left-Brain/Right-Brain Conundrum Revisited." *TheScientist.com* 18, no. 7 (2004).

———. "Handedness Develops in the Womb." *New Scientist*, 22 July 2004.

Springer, Sally P., and Georg Deutsch. *Left Brain, Right Brain*. New York: W. H. Freeman, 1993.

UCLA Press Release, "Left-Handed Persons' Brains Organized Differently than Right-Handers, UCLA Scientists Discover," 4 March 2002.

Wilson, Frank W. *The Hand: How Its Use Shapes the Brain, Language, and Human Culture*. New York: Vintage Books, 1998.

Word Detective. http://www.word-detective.com/093098.html.

Word Origins. http://www.wordorigins.org/wordors.htm.

Index